TRAVELING

WITH

GROUPS

A Guide to Planning, Preparing for and Participating in a Trip with Students or other Groups

By

Donna Day

Library of Congress Control Number: 2002095953

ISBN 0-9726059-0-8

Printed in the U.S.A. by
Morris Publishing
3212 East Highway 30
Kearney, NE 68847
1-800-650-7888

ACKNOWLEDGEMENTS

I want to express my deep appreciation to all those people who have shared their traveling experiences with me. There are so many students, parents, chaperones, instructors and many other adults that have been a part of the creation of this book that I hesitate to name them in case I leave anyone out. Others whose names I don't even know have been so helpful in their willingness to share their traveling adventures and advice for all travelers.

There are a few I do want to mention and to thank them specifically for all their help. My Mom, Vivian Wells, who engrained in me a deep love of traveling and has inspired me with her many stories of her travels around the world and with all her help in making this book possible. My three sons, Daniel, James and Jon, who provided many traveling experiences in all the group trips that I participated in with them. My daughter-in-law Rachel and friends Cathy Hefner and Bonnie Carrick for reading, editing, discussing and advising me in writing this book.

Special thanks to my husband Bob for his encouragement and advice and help in the technical aspects of this project.

This book is dedicated to my Mom, Vivian Wells, without whom this book would not have been possible.

CONTENTS

TRAVELING WITH GROUPS

A Guide to Planning, Preparing for and Participating in a Trip with Students or other Groups

INTRODUCTION:

I must commend you on your decision to consider arranging a trip and/or traveling with a group of students and/or adults. I believe traveling to be one of the most educational things anyone can possibly do. Much can be learned, both in personal growth and maturity, as well as educationally, from traveling, whether it is across the state, across the country, or across the world. It seems to me that just about every area has its own unique culture and history, sometimes similar to our own but sometimes very different. This is true even in our own United States with many differences and similarities from state to state.

Just getting away from one's familiar surroundings is very uplifting, and even more so with a well-planned trip.

The key of course, is in the planning. The suggestions and tips for designing, planning and preparing for your trip in this book will hopefully help you have a successful, safe, and enjoyable experience by being prepared mentally and physically as well as practically.

This book is aimed primarily at traveling with students but much can be applied to other groups as well. Most of the traveling suggestions can be helpful for any traveler. There are many different types of group trips, for many different age groups, but a lot of the planning and preparing is the same. Traveling with students presents rather unique situations, with special circumstances that need to be addressed and dealt with but it also brings with it many enjoyable experiences and a certain satisfaction in making it possible for many students to have a very educational and enjoyable experience. This may be an experience that many may not be able to have otherwise. My hope is that this book will encourage more people to arrange group trips with students and other groups, by providing information in the basic how to's.

PART ONE of this book is concerned primarily with the decisions made in choosing the trip and setting up all the details. It is written with the perspective of the one that has decided to create this trip for the group that he/she is specifically involved in. This person is probably a teacher, but could be a coach or another leader of any kind of group. While much of this information is geared specifically towards a student group there is still much that could be used for other groups too. Please remember that many of the examples are limited and there could be many more.

I do feel that it is very important for the "Leader" of this group to incorporate a group of adults, probably parents of the students you are involved with, in a "Trip Committee", to help you with the details and to share in the decisions that will need to be made. If your group is comprised primarily of adults it will still be helpful to include a small group of them in the planning.

After the trip is chosen and the details are being worked out I have designed a calendar of informational meetings that you can have with your large group to help them to plan and prepare for the trip. Everyone is very busy in his or her own life but they do need to take time and energy to get ready for this trip. Chances are you and your travelers will be spending quite a bit of money on this trip so you don't want it to be wasted because your group of travelers has not prepared themselves properly. This means preparing themselves mentally and physically, as well as practically.

Unfortunately sometimes problems arise, and most probably will, even on the most carefully planned trip. But if you have followed the suggestions given you may be better equipped to cope with the irritations that come up with lost luggage, misunderstandings of arrival times at housing sites, lost money, etc. and better able to have a positive attitude no matter what happens.

The calendar is designed from the perspective that your trip will take place some time in April, the usual time for Spring Break for most schools, and when most trips like this take place. However, your trip could be other times too, so you will just need to adjust the months to fit the calendar of your trip. While there are specific details (Passport, foreign currency) that you need to be concerned about with an international trip, a trip with a student and/or adult group in the United States involves many of the same details and planning.

PART TWO of the book covers the practical information needed in preparing for a major trip for anyone, with some specific information geared toward groups. Every trip is different and while you may take some different items depending upon the climate, times of year, activities you will be doing and seeing, most of the preparations will be the same. Please remember that the information included is meant to be used as suggestions on how things might be done. You will need to adjust the information to fit your group and/or yourself for your particular trip.

One thing to remember when taking a group is that no matter how much you may try to prepare them by giving everyone helpful information and guidelines they still may not follow your advice. For example, as much as you explain how important it is to carry all their extra cash in a money belt some may choose not to carry one. Only when their wallet is lost or stolen will they realize they should have followed your advice.

Unfortunately, one person's mishap may delay the whole group during the trip, and result in a lot of frustration on everybody's part.

At least with a student group you can tell them that certain things will be mandatory and that you will be checking to see if they have done the required and have prepared accordingly.

PART THREE will talk about participating in a trip and some of the things that you can expect while traveling with a group.

An Appendix at the end of the book contains copies of suggested forms that may be helpful in organizing a group trip. However, these forms are not intended, nor are they to be taken to be legal advice. They are just examples of what you might use. Please consult an attorney for your particular situation. With a school sponsored trip you would need to consult the School District's attorney for advice.

Even though this book is copyrighted I want you to feel free to use the lists, calendars, guidelines, and other items as needed. If you will be using some of the information as written please give acknowledgement as to where you got it. The forms provided will most likely need to be customized to fit your particular situation but you may use them as desired. Please check with your attorney as to the legality as they apply to your particular group.

PART ONE: PLANNING YOUR TRIP

CHAPTER 1
-
DESIGNING THE TRIP

CHOOSING THE TRIP

Now that you have decided that you would like to take a trip with a group of students, you need to decide where to go. Of course, you may already have this decided for you from your circumstances. You may be a foreign language teacher, so your choice of countries may be limited. You may be a choir director, or a band director, so are limited somewhat by available performance venues. You may be a coach, seeking a group of teams to play. You may be involved with an adult choir or symphony seeking to perform and tour overseas. You may be a part of a non-profit agency that seeks to help your group participate in a trip.

Whatever the situation, you have a big decision to make. If the decision has not already been decided for you (possibly that you have been invited to compete or perform somewhere) then you need to consider the group you want to take, when they can go, and how much they would be willing to spend. Many teachers receive all sorts of information about different tours that are offered for their specific area of interests. These can provide you with "built in" performance venues, with lots of sight-seeing on the side.

You can also put together a tour yourself. I highly recommend that you use a "Travel Agency" to help you in this, unless you are a very experienced traveler. A "Travel Agent" is especially helpful for large groups, and groups with special arrangement needs: bands with lots of instruments and uniforms, groups with lots of equipment,

GATHERING YOUR TRIP COMMITTEE

My first recommendation to you as you consider taking your particular group on a trip is to gather together a "Trip Committee" from among the parents of the students from your group or adult members from your group. The members don't necessarily need to be the same ones that are planning on going on this trip, but it would certainly be helpful. You need to advertise this "Committee" to the whole group for them to have the opportunity to volunteer to be on it, with a clear description of the amount of work and time commitment that will be needed to be on this Committee.

This is really important for you because you want everyone to have an understanding of what they are getting into, though quite honestly, you never really know until it happens. Also, many of the decisions that this Committee makes will directly impact the whole group, especially concerning the costs of the trip. For your own protection and well being, as well as the Committee's, you want the entire group of parents to know that the decisions that were made were thoroughly discussed and worked through for the benefit of the WHOLE group.

Otherwise, you may be opening yourself up to a lot of criticism and conjecture by those who don't really understand why certain decisions were made. If you have a Committee that everyone had an opportunity to be on, and that is made up of a representative set of parents/adults, and not just a "special group" that only you chose, you will be saved a lot of grief later when people start questioning why certain decisions were made. A Committee should help you as the Leader too, in being able to spread the workload so that you do not end up doing it all yourself.

COMMITTEE RESPONSIBILITIES

Your Committee meetings, probably 2 or more per month at the beginning will be spent planning and fine tuning the itinerary and discussing the arrangements for the trip. You will also be deciding on the exact cost per person, discussing the "free trips" and who gets them, and obtaining permission from the "School Board" for the trip, if needed, as well as choosing speakers and programs for the large group meetings.

Additional time may be needed to meet with the Travel Agency, school administrators, special speakers and in preparing all the paperwork needed for a large group trip.

You may want to be giving short, preliminary reports to the large group as to how things are going, and the possible costs. It will be hard to say much for sure until you have settled on many of the above decisions. You will want to get a feel from your group as to how many will be going as soon as possible. You don't want to plan on 100 students and end up with only 60 and 5 adults.

Eventually you may need only one meeting a month, either the week before or the week after your large group meeting. You also may want to meet 1/2 hour before the group meeting and 1/2 hour after the meeting with the Committee to touch base with everyone.

FIRST TRIP COMMITTEE MEETING

When you have your first meeting for parents who are interested in being on this Committee, you need to be prepared with information about trips you, and they, might be interested in, and with a description of what you expect Committee members might have to do over the next year, or two. Yes, a year and a half to two years. A trip for a group is going to probably take at least a year and a half, to two years, to plan, depending upon the size of the group, and the destination.

Not only does the planning and preparation for a group trip take quite a bit of time, but you will probably want to look at different fund raising ideas to make this trip affordable for your group of students. That way everyone will have time to save for and/or raise money for the trip.

An understanding needs to be made among the Committee members that all of the decisions that are made should focus on what is the best for the WHOLE group. Sometimes individuals may not get to do exactly what they want because whatever it is may not be good for the whole group.

Also, decisions should be made with everyone's input considered, discussed and then decided. If the rest of the parents know that the Committee did put a lot of thought into the decisions, instead of just one person forcing their desires upon all the others, the large meetings will run a lot smoother.

At this meeting your Committee will need to make some decisions as to destinations, what time of year, and a rough estimate of how much they think parents will be willing to pay. I'm sure your goal will be that all of the students in your group will be able to participate in this trip. Unfortunately not all may be able to. Sometimes a few may not be able to go due to circumstances beyond their control: parents simply not allowing them to, lack of funds, health problems, or other reasons, but hopefully the majority will be able to participate.

You will also need to determine how many adults will be going on this trip. How many will be going as chaperones, instructors, maybe a nurse/medical person, your spouse?

Also, if needed, you as the Leader need to have checked with your school administrators as to any policies that they may have concerning large group trips. They may want you to get 2 or 3 bids from different travel agencies; have you present the trip and itinerary before the School Board to receive permission to take the students; have any money collected handled through the school. They also may have a ratio of students to chaperones that they will want you to have on the trip.

If you will be using a Travel Agency you may want to contact some of your colleagues to determine if they have taken groups on trips before and which Agencies that they may have used. Sometimes packaged trips are arranged by a "Tour Company" located in another state. They will arrange for the trip and communicate with you over the phone, by fax or e-mail. At your destination a member of the Tour Company will meet you and be in contact with your group throughout your trip. An example would be specially packaged trips put on by the Disney Company. One of the band trips that I was on was arranged by a subsidiary of the Disney Company. It was called "Disney Magic Music Days" and provided performances and competitions for high school bands. There are Sports Tour Companies too, that will arrange games and competitions for your team.

At your meeting you will need to decide on which Travel Agencies to contact and who will do it, or who will be contacting a Tour Company to begin arrangements. You will need to determine a rough estimate of how many students, chaperones and staff that you will expect to be going on your trip and what price range you think your group will be willing to spend.

PLANNING YOUR TRIP

You will need to determine the travel dates. Since there are only a few times during the school year when students are able to go, you will be a bit limited to probably "Spring Break" or "Christmas Break", when students will miss the least amount of school. Sometimes foreign language classes take trips right after school is out for the summer. If the trip is held when school is in session it will probably be considered a school sponsored trip, and be under the supervision of the School Board. Some trips for 8th graders visiting Washington D.C. during Spring Break may be led by teachers but not considered to be school sponsored trips, but instead privately led trips. They would not need School Board approval, but also may have trouble publicizing the trip since the School District would not want any appearance of responsibility or liability.

You will also want to think about how long you will be able to be gone. Trips can really vary in length, but some are more desirable than others when you are traveling with a group of students. Most group trips with students are over a school vacation, usually Winter or Spring Break, so that the least amount of school is missed. A trip at these times will usually be limited to around five to eight days, which is a good amount of time to be gone. You will feel like you have had your money's worth yet most everyone will still be speaking to each other when you get back.

I would encourage you to give a lot of thought to the days before you leave on the trip and the days when you get back. If possible try to return from the trip on a Friday night if the time change for your trip is more than 3 hours. Less than that, you can probably come back on a Saturday, although one day is usually not enough to "recover" from a trip. If there is more than a 3 hour time change everyone will really feel jet lag and you need to plan accordingly. Jet lag is very real, and can really hit with a vengeance. Students may come to school on Monday, then miss several days after that when it hits. It may be even harder on adults.

Because of this you may want to plan on leaving on a Thursday or a Friday for the beginning of your trip. This will usually entail that students miss a few days of school and adults miss a few days of work, but it is usually better to plan for it at the beginning of the trip, and then have a few days to "recover" after the end of the trip.

This length of trip gives you two traveling days and five to seven days of sightseeing and performances, which is about right for most groups. Most "packaged" trips are around this length of time, with some shorter and some longer. Other trips may be longer if they are during a Summer Break when school is out. These trips will be more expensive, and you will need to consider such things as opportunities to do laundry,

Remember that in the travel industry the year is divided into "seasons". Peak season is usually considered to be late June, July and August. Off-season is mid-October through April. "Shoulder season" is May, early June and September through early October. Tours are priced accordingly. The prices can either decrease or increase depending upon the season, sometimes even weekly. If you look at a calendar of the tours offered by a Tour Company they may have a tour departing every week. The prices will rise dramatically as the peak season starts, with some changes almost weekly. Shoulder season will yield somewhat lower prices, with off-season having the lowest prices of all.

There are pros and cons to traveling in any of the seasons. Price is a big consideration, but remember that traveling in the off-season can have some drawbacks that might not be worth the difference in the costs. The weather in the off-season generally may not be the best, and may be downright miserable. Also, the days are usually shorter, so there is less daylight available for sight seeing. Some of the attractions and sights that you want to see may be closed for maintenance, or the hours they are open severely limited.

Shoulder season has a lot of advantages: lower prices, fairly good weather, smaller crowds and longer days. It is also the time when schools typically have a "Vacation Break". Some "Breaks" can be in the off-season too (March, April), which can really lower the overall cost of the trip. The weather may, or may not be an issue, depending upon where you will be going. It may actually be much more pleasant to go in the off-season if it is a place that may be very hot in the peak season (Florida, California, and Mexico).

Last, but not least, is (of course) where you will be going. Are you set on an international experience, or one in the States? There are lots of places to go, and things to see. It's just determining what you want out of the trip, and what you think everyone would be interested in, as well as what you want to accomplish on the trip (performances, classes, clinics, sightseeing, cultural and historical educational experiences, amusement parks,) When considering an international trip you do need to think about the language spoken in the countries you are visiting and if you will have someone along who speaks the language or languages. You can usually find people who speak English just about everywhere but sometimes it can be frustrating to deal with a language problem and a large group and any problems that might arise.

If you are using a Travel Agency you will need to compile all of this information so that they can give you an accurate bid estimate. Once you get estimates you will then be able to determine if the trip price is within your price range. From there you will be able to do some negotiating on the final itinerary. A lot of this may be subject to change as you and your Committee discusses the estimates. If you are bound by a school policy that you must get other bids then you will have to do that. However, if you find a Travel Agency that has experience with your type of group, especially if part of your situation concerns setting up performances and shipping a lot of instruments, you may want to try to go with them if you are unsure about the other Agencies abilities in these areas. In the Appendix there is a chart to help you determine your trip parameters and provide an easy way to compare bids from various Tour Agencies as you ask them to provide their bid and suggestions.

Other Agencies that want to gain experience in working with large groups may be more willing to negotiate with your group, and even give up some of their commission, in order to win your bid. It's perfectly OK to go with them too, if you feel comfortable with them. You and your Committee will need to give the estimates a lot of thought, and hopefully, will not simply go with whoever has the lowest bid.

FINE TUNING THE ITINERARY

At first you may get a preliminary itinerary from your Travel Agent with sight seeing spots, performances and housing sites suggested, along with departure and arrival flights and times. Hopefully your Travel Agent will be familiar with moving a large group from place to place, along with the amount of time performances take, including set-up and take-down, so your itinerary will allow enough time for this. If this is new to your Agent you will want to make sure to inform him/her of the amount of time you would estimate the performances would take. Also, you may need to allow some time in your schedule for practice times. You will need time and space for these.

You will then want to "fine tune" the itinerary to fit your group specifically. Maybe there are other things that your group would like to see, either in addition to what has been suggested, or in place of. Also, with a student group you might want to allow time for some "fun" things (water slides, amusement parks, Hard Rock Café visit) that a totally adult group might not be interested in.

You will definitely want to consider the amount of "free time" available to your travelers. With an adult group this is usually not a problem, but with a student group you need to consider all of the available time and what the students will be doing. Too much "free time" such as evenings in hotels after dinner with nothing planned could possibly be an invitation to problems.

What usually works for most student groups is to have events planned in the evenings, such as night tours, theater visits, performances or practices, so that you do not return to your housing site until an hour or so from the "bed-check" time. This way everyone has a little time to call home from the public phone if needed, to buy snacks at the hotel, and of course, socialize. If you are leaving the housing site the next morning you might want to give them a little extra time to pack, though probably they will just wait until after the "bed-check" time anyway. Moving up the "bed-check" time might be helpful on these nights, to give them a little extra sleep time.

Keeping a rather "packed" itinerary may be pretty tiring but it will keep everybody busy and provide fewer chances for anyone to get into trouble.

Most of the time you will move as a group from sight to sight. Sometimes however there may be times to break into smaller groups for meals or shopping. You will need to determine if a chaperone needs to be with the smaller groups all the time or if it will be OK for students to be in small groups by themselves, or a combination, depending upon the situation.

Airline Package

The airline part of a tour usually is only the airline costs for the whole group. A Travel Agent will negotiate with the airline as to the total costs, including all seats, any upgrades, and any "free" seats. If your group is large, over 50 or so, you may have to have two or three separate flights for your whole group. You may even end up with different airlines for different parts of your group. The bottom line for this is that the airline needs to make money, and prices on seats vary a whole lot, depending upon when the tickets were purchased. An airline may try to give you a good price, but they can only give you a limited amount of seats per flight at that price.

Try to get the flights as close together as possible. This will help with the transportation to and from the airport. If they have to be several hours apart you will need to arrange for separate transportation to the airport and possibly to the housing site. Sometimes a flight may leave later but arrive before another flight that left earlier, depending upon flight plans and layovers!

"Land" Package

The "Land" portion of your trip usually can include the transportation from the airport to your housing site on arrival and then for departure, tour buses for any transportation thereafter, housing, security, any provided meals, tour guides, and entrances to museums, sites, attractions, entertainment, or special tours. Any or all of which may or may not be arranged by your Travel Agent and included in the total price quoted to you by the Travel Agency. You may arrange some of this separately from the "Tour Package", and pay for it separately, but usually the Travel Agency will make most of the arrangements. The Travel Agency should also arrange for any Visa's that you may need when entering foreign countries.

When considering entertainment be sure it is age appropriate to your group. Some theater productions may not be suitable for younger students.

Transportation to and from the airport may be slightly different from the tour buses you will use throughout the trip because of scheduling and the closeness of the airport to your housing site. Also, if you will be coming on different flights, you may be arriving and departing at different times, and you may have different sizes of buses for each group.

Tour Guides

When you arrange for tour bus transportation you may or may not have the option of having tour guides accompany your group. Tour guides are especially helpful in non-English speaking countries, but can be helpful wherever you go. Bus drivers should be concentrating on driving so they will not be able talk. If your Travel Agent is traveling with you he or she can be very helpful, although he or she may not know a lot of the history of the areas you are visiting, and can only be on one bus at a time.

Since you probably consider this trip to be an educational experience you should consider the issue of hiring tour guides very carefully. While it is an additional expense they can be extremely helpful and provide a lot of important information. If you do not arrange to have tour guides, your group may not be able to really experience or comprehend some of the sites and things they will be seeing. They may not really understand the history or importance of what they are viewing, and may even miss seeing some things simply because they didn't know what to look for.

Tour guides would be on **each** of your tour buses as you travel through the areas you are visiting. They would describe the areas and talk about the history. When you arrive at a historical site the guide should tell you a little bit about it and what specific things to be sure to look for. They will stay with your group throughout the time you are sightseeing and continue to talk about it, unless you have arranged for a specific guided tour at that site.

If you are visiting more than one country you may need to have different tour guides in each country, according to that particular country's laws. Your Travel Agent will arrange for all of this.

I have been on trips with tour guides and on trips without tour guides. I personally prefer having a tour guide, even though it does make the trip more expensive. It is very frustrating to look back on a trip and feel that I could have learned much more about a country's history and culture if I would have had someone explaining some of it and pointing out specific things to observe and look for throughout the trip.

There may also be special guided tours of a town, museum, special feature (Westminster Abbey, for example) that you may want to arrange for your group. Your Travel Agent should discuss with you what is available. Sometimes the guided tours are the only way you can see the attraction. There are usually fees for these tours, for which your Travel Agent can arrange payment, so that each traveler doesn't have to carry additional money to cover them during the trip

One thing to remember with any tour guide is that he/she will be describing and explaining everything from his or her perspective. Specifically, from his or her country's historical, cultural and political point of view. The tour guide has been taught under his or her country's educational system, which may, or may not be pro-America.

This can be a bit unnerving to students who have only been taught from the American perspective and who may have never heard anyone speak with strong convictions from a different perspective than the one that they have been taught.

Be sure to remind your travelers of this so they will take all they hear with a big grain of salt. Remind them that they shouldn't challenge or disagree with the tour guide's statements but listen politely. They aren't going to change the tour guide's perspective, and may instead appear to be very rude. They can talk about it later with just the group present to gain an understanding of the different perspectives.

I would suggest that in the preparatory meetings for the trip that information about the history, culture and sights you will be seeing and the itinerary be presented, with handouts given to help educate everyone involved with the trip. This will go a long way in helping everyone to have a more enjoyable and educational trip.

"Free Trips"

One area full of problems has to do with "free trips". Many times a Tour Company will offer "free trips" as an incentive for "Leaders" to put together trips. Usually the offer is 1 free trip per 15 paid trips. You as the Leader, and your Committee, need to remember that there is no such thing as a "free trip". Especially now, when there are so many tours offered, and airlines have no trouble in filling their planes. However, having said that, there are ways that you can work out "deals" with your Tour Company or Travel Agency.

Usually the Leader receives a free trip no matter what, just because the Agency wants your business. The Agency then offers you a certain amount of "free trips" per amount of paid trips that you put together. The more people on the trip the greater the commission for the Agency. Your question to the Agency must be that if you don't use them can that make the trip cheaper for everyone else and by how much?

You may want the Agency to provide an "inspection trip" of a few days for the Leader and one or two others to "check out" the housing, venues, and sights a few months before the actual trip. This can be very helpful.

Sometimes the Agency may not be able to get any "free" airline tickets, so they just raise the total price of each individual trip to cover the cost of the "free" ones. They may get free items on the land package however. Sometimes hotels will actually give extra free rooms because you purchase a certain amount of rooms from them. Amusement parks often give extra tickets too, when a certain number are purchased.

Another area where money can be saved, or not, has to do with the tour buses you may be using. A tour bus usually holds around 50 people. This is fine, unless you have say 75 people on your tour. 2 buses are going to cost the same if you have 51 people, or 100 people. The cost **per person** however, will be lower with the 100 people.

With all of this you may want to take some, or all, of the "free trips", but you may not want to give them as totally free. You might charge them 1/2 to 2/3 of the total amount everyone is paying. You could then offer these trips to chaperones, instructors, your spouse (with consent of the Committee), and to needy students in the form of scholarships. You may want to have an application form for this. In negotiating with the Agency you may agree that the "free trips" airline portion is paid for, and the land package is somewhat reduced. This will in turn boost the total number of paid fares going, and increases the Agency's commission, but not really "hurt" anyone because the land portion is greatly reduced.

Here is an example:

115 students
15 chaperones
1 leader
1 nurse/medical person
3 staff
135 total

135 paid airlines = 9 free (1 per 15)

$1500 total trip cost ($600 airline cost) 21 can pay only $1000 – which will cover the $600 in airline cost plus $400 in extra costs (Leader and the Nurse/medical person go totally free)

This means 15 chaperones, 3 staff, and 3 students pay $1000 instead of $1500.

This is a very touchy situation that must be thoroughly discussed. Much must be considered, especially how much work is actually expected from those receiving discounted trips. There is a lot of extra time and work involved in a trip like this, so it is reasonable to give discounted tickets to the adults going, although it is not required nor should it automatically be expected. This is also a way to help needy students to go on this trip, as well as staff helpers who may not be able to afford the trip, not to mention chaperones.

Totally free trips may cause a lot of dissension in the large group as a whole. If the $1000 cost is too high for the staff maybe additional help can be given to them from the Committee. Scholarships from other sources may be found for other needy students. Our Band Booster group was able to give four $500 and one $400 scholarship for the England trip.

The Leader's spouse may be offered a discounted trip too, if he or she is helping with a lot of the preparations for the trip, and possibly chaperoning too. However, this needs to be done with a lot of discussion with the Committee. If this is a school sponsored trip you will need to check on this because the School District may not allow it anyway. You do not want your Leader to get into trouble with the School District just because you wanted to be nice and give his/her spouse a discounted trip.

The Leader's trip should be totally free, since they are ultimately the one responsible for the trip, as well as the one who is doing a lot of extra work and spending a lot of time on this project.

It is highly recommended that a person in the position of nurse/medical person should be along. It is very helpful if they have some first aid/medical training, and that it is understood that if someone becomes sick on the trip then they are the logical one to stay with the sick person, and possibly miss that day's activities. They are also "on call" **all of the time** for sicknesses and injuries, and may have to dispense prescription drugs according to your School District policies. This person should also receive a totally free trip because of the situation of being "on call".

In any case, you should get estimates from the Travel Agency for the cost of the trip with, and without, any "free trips" and/or discounted trips. You need to consider how much the addition of these trips adds to the total cost per person for the trip. It may be that in the end everyone would rather have the cost lowered for everyone going on the trip, rather that offering discounted trips. Do consider the fact that it is possible that some of those who might be receiving the discounted trips might not be able to go on the trip at all if they do not receive some sort of discount or scholarship. This may in turn throw off the cost of the trip by lowering the number of people actually going on the trip, lowering the number of chaperones and staff you will have and the number of students able to participate in the trip. There are lots of things to consider in making these decisions.

Others on the Trip

There are other situations where additional people might want to go on your trip. Sometimes chaperones will want the whole family to go on the trip, including brothers and sisters. A husband and wife should have any siblings of the student stay in the room with them, not with the student. It puts the students in an awkward position if they have to have younger children staying in the room with them and should not be allowed. In addition, if parents want to bring their other children, one of them should not be a chaperone of the students. They will need to be looking after their own child or children and should not be distracted by other responsibilities.

I have seen these situations occur and they have created hard feelings and misunderstandings. The parent is distracted trying to keep the child happy because they are bored, tired, mad, and then the parent can't be a good chaperone. The students feel neglected or they don't want to bother the chaperone because they see that they are busy with the child.

Another situation would be if other people just want to come on the trip. They may or may not be related to the students but they want to come, but not chaperone. They may view it as a special opportunity to travel and don't mind being with a student group.

This can be a tricky situation especially if you need a few more people on your trip to help make it a little cheaper for everyone. Some groups have handled this by having the "extra" people pay more for the trip. If you are giving a price break to the chaperones by reducing their overall cost and/or giving them rooms for two without an extra charge you could charge the "extras" this additional charge, or maybe even more.

Another group I know actually charged these "extra" travelers a few hundred dollars more and used this extra money to help out with scholarships for needy students. In this particular case the trip was a very special one with that particular group being one of the first to visit China from this state. Certain dignitaries (mayor, principal) wanted to go too, and be a part of the experience.

In situations like these you need to thoroughly discuss this with the Committee and those wishing to go. They need to understand that they will be with the group and will not be able to go off on their own. There might be exceptions to this such as activities planned just for them but if they are traveling with your group they need to remember that they need to participate in the group's activities, and not demand special privileges. The trip is first and foremost for the students!!!

Housing Costs

Another area you need to consider in the costs of the trip are the individual room charges for housing. The types of housing you may be using could be hotels, youth hostels, university dorm rooms, home stays with local families and even sleeping on gym floors. The charges will vary widely depending upon what you choose. You may even have a combination of these.

With hotel stays students usually stay in groups of four, while adults are usually in twos. It is much more comfortable for adults this way and respectful of their needs. Unfortunately, a hotel will usually have different charges for rooms for two, three and four. You will need to consider all this in your planning with the Travel Agent and make sure that you have allowed enough for all the housing costs. Hopefully when you make these decisions you will know the exact number of adults and students that will be going on the trip. This will help in planning how many rooms will be needed and the costs involved before you decide on the overall cost per person for the trip.

Be sure to discuss room assignments with the chaperones going. Couples will want to be together, but sometimes there are adults who want to be by themselves. Also, you may come out with an odd number of adults and/or students. Because of this you may need to put the students or adults in a room for three.

Possibly this is a way to "reward" the adults going on this trip by putting them in rooms of two. The extra costs will be spread out in the overall cost of the trip per person. This is especially nice if you are unable to give a price break to the adults otherwise.

If this becomes an issue of contention you may need to ask all the adults to pay the additional costs of having rooms for two or three and especially if they want a room by themselves. Single rooms always cost more.

In **NO** case should you ever have one adult in a room with students. Only in situations of "cabin" style housing of usually six or more students would you have adults in the same room, and you would **ALWAYS** have two adults in the room together with the students. This is for everyone's protection.

Youth hostels may have rooms holding four up to fourteen or more. You will need to decide on the chaperone assignment for these, but usually the costs are the same per person, regardless of the number per room. Though be sure to check with the hostels for the exact charges. Sometimes hostels may charge less if you bring your own sheet. A "sheet sack", which is a sheet sewn together so it forms a bag, with a cover for a pillow, may be purchased here and taken with you. Be sure to check on the differences in costs if you bring your own sheets, or not.

Home stays with local families in the areas you are visiting may be an inexpensive option. However, these do take a lot of coordinating on the part of the people you will be visiting, and may not be feasible with a large group. Usually you would have two students together and two adults together. Home stay families may provide some meals too. Be sure you have clear communication with the Home stay Coordinator about what is being provided. Home stays can be a wonderful way to really learn about the culture of the country as well as meet "regular people" that you may not be able to otherwise.

The charges for a trip may change to fit your individual situations, and the willingness of your Travel Agency to work with you. They may be willing to give up some of their commission to have your business. Also, if you have a parent Booster Group, they may be able to cover some of the extra expenses, (security, renting instruments) so that the total cost is reduced for everyone.

Security

Security can be a big issue with students. You will need to check at each housing site as to what kind of security is provided. Hotels will sometimes contract with a security group if they have a lot of student groups staying there. You will have to arrange for this with the hotel and the costs will usually be included with the housing bill and paid for through your Travel Agency or you may contract to pay for them separately from the Travel Agency bill.

The security guards usually go on duty at an agreed upon time (possibly 11:00PM to 6:00AM) when you have your bed check. Chaperones would go from room to room checking to see that all students are in their own rooms. After that students are to stay in their rooms until "wake up" time. Security guards then sit in the hallways and make sure the students do not come out of their rooms, and no one else tries to get in. The latter is especially important if there are other students in the hotel. It is money well spent.

Otherwise the chaperones and/or staff will need to do the "policing" of the halls, usually for a few hours late at night when everyone is really tired.

Sometimes, hired security guards are not available. You are going to have to decide how to handle these situations. We will discuss this in a later chapter.

Renting and Transporting Instruments

If your group is a band or orchestra with a lot of instruments you will need to discuss transporting the instruments thoroughly with your Travel Agent. Airlines may charge extra for additional instruments and shipping containers if there is more than one item per person going on the trip. They may charge extra or may give you a weight limit and charge if you go over this. Don't forget to think about all the extra things that you might need, including uniforms, costumes, music stands, props, supplies, and try to determine how many containers you will need.

Sometimes the airline may want you to bring all the instruments and shipping containers down the day before your flight. They will be x-rayed and put on your plane ahead of time. This will be very helpful on the day of your flight. One less thing to worry about on a busy day.

Smaller instruments and other items may travel better in shipping containers rather than by themselves. Make lists of everything.

You might want to consider renting some of the instruments in the country where you will be visiting. This may save on wear and tear on your instruments, especially the large ones, and on shipping costs.

Don't forget to include a way of transporting the instruments, props, shipping containers once you get to your destination and on your tour. You may need to rent a truck and driver to haul all of your instruments around. There probably will not be room for them on your tour buses.

Remember to bring any tools and supplies that you need to assemble music stands and instruments, props. If you must tape shut the latches on the cases for the flights include lots of extra duct tape for the return trip. A luggage tag and/or label needs to be attached or taped to each case or box. Locks are OK but be sure there are at least two sets of **labeled** keys! Be sure to arrange for a locked storage area at your housing sites.

Include a sewing kit and extra parts if uniforms or costumes have a lot of pieces to them. Items can easily get lost, or even just dropped in the mud right before a performance. If your group wears gloves for performances be sure to bring extras.

Sports Equipment and Uniforms

If yours is a sports team you will need to consider all the different equipment you will need. You will have to decide how much you may have to bring and what may be supplied at your destinations and competitions. Also consider what uniforms, warm-ups, shoes, your players will need and if they will need more than one set. You will need to decide what items you might want your individual players to pack themselves (personal mitts, batting gloves, uniforms, warm-ups, shoes) and what large items you may need to pack in shipping crates (balls, nets, catcher's gear, bats).

Depending upon how much equipment you will need, you may need an extra vehicle for transporting it. You may be able to carry all your equipment on your tour buses if the containers aren't too heavy or take up very much space.

Extra Costs

You may have additional costs that are not part of the basic Travel Agency costs. Their costs usually include the airline fares, transportation from the airport to your destination and back to the airport at the end of your trip, tour bus transportation throughout the trip, tour guides, all housing, possibly some meals, museum fees, tours, attractions, entertainment, and theatre tickets.

Other trip costs you must consider may include bus transportation from your location (school) to the airport and back again at the end of the trip, extra shipping costs, equipment transportation costs during the tour, rental car costs (gas, tolls) that may not be covered by the Travel Agency, housing security, special imprinted shirt commemorating the trip, and printing costs for handouts.

A local Travel Agency may cover all or some of these costs with the total fee charged per person. If you are using a national Agency you may have to collect and pay for most of these other costs. For example:

Travel Agency $1400
Includes airline costs, tour bus transportation, housing, entrances into museums and attractions, 12 meals, theatre tickets, some security, tour guides

Other Trip Costs $100
Includes bus to and from airport, shipping costs, paperwork and printing, door prizes, special shirts, instrument rental

You collect all the money, then send the Travel Agency their share, and you arrange and pay for the other costs.

Meals

It is better to try to give an idea of all the costs involved in a trip like this when you first present it to the group, if at all possible, than to have complaints later when they realize there are other costs involved that weren't apparent when the estimated trip cost was first presented. However, sometimes unforeseen extra costs may come up later so be sure to tell them this and that you have tried to come as close as possible. Be **very clear** about what meals will be provided in the main payment, and what meals are not. Extra money will be necessary, and this must be budgeted for from the very beginning. Snacks and beverages will always need to be budgeted for because there will always be a need for a least a few snacks, beverages, and possibly bottled water on any kind of trip.

It can be deceiving when a trip for 7 days is described as costing **only** $950, but in reality, only 2 meals are provided. The extra $250 or so needed for meals and snacks may come as a surprise, and not a welcome one, for those not totally aware of what is happening.

Usually you can get breakfast provided at your housing site for a reasonable cost. At times a hotel provided breakfast might seem a little expensive. You will have to consider what kind of breakfast is provided, if students will actually eat it, and if there are other restaurants and fast food places near by. If your students would prefer fast food type breakfasts and they are readily available this might be a good alternative.

However, since it is strongly suggested that students and adults get a good breakfast, having one at the housing site that has already been paid for is very desirable, especially if you are not sure what is available nearby. Some students may not want to take the extra time to walk somewhere else to eat, they'd rather sleep, but they will come down for a breakfast if they don't have to walk very far. Sometimes they will not want to spend the extra money for breakfast, but in the long run they will usually end up spending the same, or more for food, as they eat the rest of the day. Unfortunately some will eat just snacks and end up getting very cranky from lack of "good" food.

Be sure to find out what type of breakfast is provided. A "Continental" style breakfast usually only includes rolls, jam, juice, coffee and tea. An "American or English" style will also have eggs, bacon, sausage, cereal, and bread.

Sometimes dinners maybe available at youth hostels. This is another meal that may be able to be included in your overall cost. Hostels can often supply packed lunches for your group too. These might come in handy if there is not a good lunch stop on your sightseeing tour. Home stay families may, or may not, provide dinners and/or breakfasts. This all needs to be discussed very carefully with the Home stay Coordinator. Be sure this is clearly understood by all involved before the trip is finalized with all the costs carefully considered, along with the convenience for the entire group.

It may be possible to arrange for other meals to be provided for by making arrangements at special restaurants (Hard Rock Café), amusements park meal vouchers, and don't forget meals on airplanes.

A suggestion here: try to get as many meals as possible provided in the main trip. This is easier on everyone's budget, and reduces the amount of extra cash needed for the trip. It is also much easier for students, and adults, to not have to manage that much cash on the trip.

You may not want to carry a lot of cash at one time, but then you are dependent upon finding an ATM machine. This can be a lot more difficult because you do not have a lot of freedom to roam around when you are with a large group of students and adults on a strict itinerary. ATM's are becoming more prevalent everywhere now, but you may not have enough time for 100 people to use an ATM machine before dinner.

Again, snacks and beverages are something that will need to be budgeted for because everyone will need at least some snacks, beverages, and possibly bottled water on the trip. You can take some snacks with you from home: granola bars, trail mix, a bottle or two of water, but you will probably need to buy some on your trip. Don't forget to budget for this!

WHO GOES ON THE TRIP

Students

There is a touchy issue of which students will actually be allowed to go on this trip. You need to point out to everyone interested that this trip is a privilege, not a right. There may be students who are either too immature to be able to handle the responsibilities involved in participating in a trip like this, or some that by their previous behavior give you cause for concern that they may not obey the rules when they are on the trip. Also, there may be students who have certain medical conditions that may cause concern.

These situations can be addressed in different ways. Those with medical conditions need to meet with the Leader and discuss how the medical condition may be managed so that they can participate in the trip. Maybe they will simply need to get additional rest, or have someone help them manage their wheelchair. In any case, discussion needs to take place to determine if a parent will be required to go on the trip to help.

It is really too much to ask a chaperone to assume this kind of responsibility, and to give up their time on the trip to stay back at the housing site or on the bus with someone who needs to. (It is a different situation in dealing with students who become sick on the trip, which will be dealt with later.) There is no reason that these students should not be allowed to participate in the trip, but parents must assume the responsibility here. Parents and students need to be very up front about their medical conditions and explain the situation fully with the Leader and medical person on the trip and describe any help they will need.

Concerns about students' behavior are another matter. The Leader should meet with the parents and the student and discuss the concerns about inappropriate behavior, what changes need to be made, and the consequences if changes are not made. Non-refundability of payments should be discussed relating to the occasion that the student's behavior prevents them from going on the trip after payments have been made.

Immaturity in students is a little harder to address. Students coming into high school may seem very immature, and unable to handle a trip like this. But with proper preparation, and just "growing up" a little in the 7 or so months until the trip takes place may produce wonders in their maturity level. This is an educational opportunity and a learning experience for all. However, there may be some individuals who simply are so immature that they will not be able to handle the pressures and responsibilities involved with traveling in a large group without their parents. Again, the chaperones are not surrogate parents here, and are not to be expected to assume total responsibility for someone else's child.

Chaperones

You will pretty much have to accept who signs up to chaperone unless there are major concerns about a person. If it is a school sponsored trip the School District may have a "volunteer form" which they will want everyone to fill out. This may even include a "background check" run through the State and Local Police Departments, and may even need to be fingerprinted. If a person does not "pass" this, the School District may not allow them to chaperone. Otherwise it is very difficult to turn someone down to chaperone, especially if they are paying their own way.

However, if you have major concerns about a chaperone's ability to cope with students on a large group trip you will need to discuss this privately with that particular person.

If it appears that you will have a lot more people volunteering to chaperone than you really need you may want to have some sort of application form that everyone fills out and then the Leader and/or the Committee will make the selections. If there is room for "extras" to come on the trip, but not chaperone, you may want to consider encouraging those that are not chosen to chaperone to consider coming along but not chaperoning. However, if this is your situation you will need to be very careful here. Chaperones need a least a few "perks" or they will simply want to be "extras" and you will end up without enough chaperones.

Asking those chosen to chaperone other group events may be helpful in preparing them for chaperoning on a major trip.

Health problems may be another concern and as the Leader you may want to discuss any concerns you might have if you know that particular person has health problems. Trips like this can be very strenuous and everyone needs to be able to keep up. The England trip I was on there was a gentleman who had by-pass surgery several months before the trip. He was all healed by the departure date and had a great time on the trip.

The schedule needs to be discussed thoroughly with all adults interested in going on the trip, and all the demands that will be expected of chaperones need to be clearly explained.

Once the chaperones have been decided upon you will want to involve them in the discussions about the trip and participate in helping with the meetings. Chaperones and students need opportunities to get to know each other before the trip begins.

It is really important for the Leader to express appreciation for those chaperoning as many times as possible. Chaperones have the opportunity to go on a trip, possibly to foreign countries which they might not otherwise get to visit, and maybe at a reduced cost. However, there are a lot of responsibilities involved with chaperoning students as well as a lack of freedom to "just do what you want". Chaperones need and deserve a lot of appreciation. It is a lot harder job than it may appear to be.

MEDICAL CONCERNS IN FOREIGN COUNTRIES AND THE U.S.

Most of the countries you will be visiting will not have any major medical concerns. However it is always good to check with the Centers for Disease Control. They can give you health information about the specific destinations you will be visiting as well as general health tips for traveling. There is also information on vaccination recommendations for travelers of all ages. Their web site is www.cdc.gov/travel/. Be sure to check this when you are planning your trip, and present this information to your group. If there are a lot of concerns in this area you may want to arrange for a doctor or nurse to speak to your group about this and how everyone can keep themselves healthy while traveling.

Sometimes there are medical concerns for certain regions in the United States too, such as mosquito and tick problems. Be sure to check on this.

Adequate medical insurance coverage needs to be addressed, with additional trip medical insurance thoroughly discussed in your group meetings. Everyone needs to be aware of the type of medical care offered in the countries you will be visiting too, so you may have to do some research on this, as well as discussing it with your Travel Agent.

Travel Insurance

You will also want to make clear to the participants which payments, if any, will be refundable if they have to cancel their trip and what reasons will be allowed for refunds. You will also want to explain the possible additional cost of Travel Insurance. Travel Insurance is usually paid for when the trip is booked with a non-refundable payment. It usually costs around 5 to 8% of the cost of the trip and is provided by the Travel Agency. This will probably need to be bought at the time of your first payment, but the timing will be up to your Travel Agent. Travel Insurance is usually paid to the Travel Agency directly, but may be "packaged" with the total payment to the Travel Agency. Each family will need to make this decision for themselves unless you provide the insurance in a "package" with the other trip costs.

You should have a special meeting (probably in September) with everyone interested in this trip and the Travel Agent, so that the Agent can thoroughly explain Travel Insurance and exactly what it covers. It is very important that this insurance is clearly explained, and discussed.

Typically, Travel Insurance covers the refundablilty of certain portions of the payments to the Travel Agent (airfare, hotel costs) if you need to cancel your trip for acceptable reasons, as well as medical insurance for medical and dental emergencies in a foreign country. It will be helpful if the Agent brings brochures and applications for the Travel Insurance and then arranges for payment a few days later, after parents have had a chance to check their own insurance coverage. A lot will depend on the availability of good medical care in the countries you are visiting (Travel Insurance will usually pay for a medical evacuation if it is deemed necessary). Even with good medical care you may need to be flown home in a sick or injured state, and this may not be covered by your own medical insurance. Most personal medical insurance policies will cover you overseas, however Medicare does not. Usually you have to pay for the medical expenses there and then be reimbursed when you get home. This could be a very expensive proposition.

Everyone will need to weigh the need for trip cancellation insurance too. When booking a trip this far out you won't know if you or a family member may become ill, and prevent you from traveling. Also, there may be some protection here to cover your expenses if your Tour Company or airline goes out of business or someone in the Company or Agency steals the payments that have been made. This has happened!

Usually these types of insurance (medical and trip cancellation) are sold together as Trip/Travel Insurance but you can talk to your Agent to see if there is any way to buy them separately.

Trip/Travel Insurance needs to be carefully considered by the Leader and the Committee while planning the trip. This insurance could become very important when traveling with students and other groups too, especially with members who may be in less than optimal health and/or elderly. You never know when someone may become extremely ill, or even just fall getting off the bus and break a leg. The issue of adequate medical coverage then becomes **very** important.

A Leader of a group will want to know that every person has adequate medical coverage anyway because he or she does not want to be responsible for anyone on a trip who does not have some sort of medical insurance. You will want to ask that everyone show proof of some type of medical insurance coverage when they sign up for the trip.

It is possible that the Leader and Committee will feel that everyone should have Travel Insurance covering medical insurance and trip cancellation insurance so that there are no problems if anything unfortunate happens to anyone on the trip. If this is the case the Committee may ask the Travel Agency to offer a "package" deal with the cost of the Travel Insurance included in the entire cost of the trip being offered by the Travel Agency. Sometimes this is the easiest way to go to make sure everyone is covered and can relieve a lot of worries concerning these areas.

If you do provide this "package" deal be sure to explain what portions of the payments are nonrefundable. Some of the expenses your group may be providing may be nonrefundable, such as paperwork, transportation to the airport and back, commemorative shirt, and other items that are not covered by the Trip/Travel Insurance Policy. Your Committee will need to decide what amounts will be refundable, if any, so you want to clearly describe what portion of the payments will be nonrefundable if someone has to cancel their trip.

About a month before the Band Trip that I went on to Mexico a friend of my oldest son Daniel had appendicitis. He was planning to go on that trip and luckily was recovered enough to be able to go. We were happy for him and also relieved that it had not happened on the trip. In both situations Travel Insurance would have helped immensely. If he had not been able to go on the trip at least some of the payments would have been refunded. If he had become ill there the medical portion of the insurance would have been a big help.

At this point in time you will also want to check the coverage offered by the Travel Insurance concerning the situation of terrorist attacks. You will want to know if you will be covered if a terrorist attack causes your trip to be cancelled, or if an attack causes such fear that you want to cancel your own trip. Be sure the description of the coverage is very clear on these particular issues.

Other Types of Insurance

Other types of insurance may be needed when traveling. If you will be taking personal band or orchestra instruments each traveler will need to find out if they already have, or may need to purchase additional insurance to cover their instruments. Some may already have insurance that will cover their instrument as part of their homeowner's insurance. Others may have added a rider onto their homeowner's policy to cover especially valuable instruments (example: violin, cello, French Horn).

Encourage everyone to consider their situation very carefully and to check into their personal insurance coverage. Traveling is very hard on instruments and there is always the possibility of theft. If they do not have insurance or have an inadequate amount they need to consider adding it.

With a school sponsored trip there should be adequate insurance coverage for the school owned instruments, but this insurance would not cover personally owned instruments. A city orchestra or symphony will have insurance on the instruments owned by that particular group, but again, not on those instruments that are personally owned. Remind your travelers not to **assume** that their instruments are covered by insurance, they need to check with their insurance company.

The Leader needs to check on insurance coverage for any sports equipment, props, costumes, or uniforms that may be taken on the trip too. If you are taking special uniform cases, shipping crates and boxes you need to check on coverage for these items also. These items can be very expensive to replace.

The insurance company for the School District or "city" orchestra, symphony, may ask for a detailed list of the items being taken on the trip, the exact itinerary and the specific departure and return dates sent to them.

Insurance for lost baggage, loss, damage, or theft of personal items (camera, jewelry, electronic items) needs to be considered too. Usually there is some coverage with a homeowner's policy but an additional rider may be needed for expensive items. Everyone needs to check on his or her coverage.

If someone in the group will be driving while on the trip, especially if they might be driving a rental truck containing instruments, uniforms, props or other items, be sure that person has checked with their insurance company and explained what they will be doing. Additional coverage may need to be purchased for the trip.

Discuss with your Travel Agent what type of driver's license will be necessary for your particular situation.

SCHOLARSHIPS

You may have a group that is working with your travelers, a Booster Group, or even your Committee, that may want to give Scholarships to your students. You will need to decide upon the amount of each Scholarship that you want to give, how many you can give, and what criteria that you want to include in your application process. You may want to have a small Scholarship Committee create the application and then choose the recipients after reviewing the completed applications.

It is very important that you let everyone know about the availability of the Scholarships, the application process, the due date and any limitations put on the Scholarships.

The Committee I was involved with for the England Trip decided that those applying needed to commit to going on the trip if they received the Scholarship. We needed to be sure that they would be able to afford the rest of the costs of the trip if they received the Scholarship, and not cancel out later on. When the Scholarship Committee decided upon the recipients a member of that Committee called the recipients with congratulations, and confirmed that they would be able to go on the trip. If someone would have said no, that they would not be able to go on the trip even with the Scholarship, then the Committee could have awarded that Scholarship to someone else. This was done in case their circumstances had changed since they had filled out their application.

We also had the "Award Date" of the Scholarships before the first payment was due so that the recipients would know they were receiving the Scholarships and could commit to going on the trip. However, they could not use the Scholarship for the first payment.

The Scholarship Committee for our group consisted of the three people who had been elected to award College Scholarships for our Band Booster group. The Trip Scholarship Applications were patterned after the College Scholarship Applications. The scoring guide was very similar to what was used for the College Scholarships also, with a few changes.

Calls were made to the recipients of the Scholarships and letters of "Congratulations" sent. Letters of regret were also sent to those that did not receive Scholarships so that they would know.

You will need to decide upon the procedures you will use for your particular group of travelers. This can be a very rewarding experience to those involved with a deep sense of satisfaction on being able to make it possible for someone to go on a trip. See the Appendix for the sample Scholarship Application and additional suggestions.

A WORD ABOUT TERRORISM

September 11, 2001 affected many, many things in the lives of Americans, as well as all the citizens of the world. Unfortunately, that devastating event made everyone much more worried about traveling anywhere. This is so sad because traveling, no matter where you go, expands your horizons and broadens your thinking in a way that no amount of just reading or watching a video of the area ever could.

The fear of a terrorist attack **should not** stop you from traveling. However, you should always be very well prepared wherever you travel. In planning your trip you need to think about the areas you want to visit and consider if it is really wise to travel there with a large group. Most countries should be just fine, but if you have any doubts you need to talk this over with your Travel Agent. You can also check the State Department's Travel advisories at http://travel.state.gov/travel_warnings.html for further advice.

When my son Daniel and I were planning on participating in an 8th Grade Trip to Washington D.C. our country was in the midst of the Persian Gulf War. As the tensions increased some of the parents were concerned about their children visiting our Nation's Capital at such a difficult time, and some even considered canceling the trip for their child.

The Travel Agency assured us that they were in contact with the authorities in each of the areas that we planned on visiting and would let us know of any precautions that we would need to take.

Security was heightened in the Federal buildings that we visited: more metal detectors and armed guards, but we were able to take all the tours that we had been scheduled for. I think that the heightened awareness of the World situation made the tour of our Nation's Capital even more meaningful to us in some ways.

In any case, it is very important that all your travelers be well organized in their travel preparations, and need to stay informed about what is happening in the World in general. They also need to be reminded that they will need to be patient with the additional security measures in airports, major sights and museums.

To reassure the parents at home it may be more important now than ever for everyone to try to call home a few times during the trip. An email sent periodically from the Leader to a "distribution list" of all the parents and other interested persons several times during the trip might relieve a lot of fears too.

CHAIN OF COMMAND

One thing that may be helpful for your group is to design a chart showing the "chain of command" that is governing your particular group. There is a chart in the Appendix that may help you with this. Many times groups like to know how the decision making process works concerning your group and who is responsible to whom.

A group is usually, but not always, governed by some type of Board of Directors. The Board may be a private group, a school district, or maybe a non-profit agency. This group may provide direction, funding, competitions, games (such as Little League) and other things.

The Board may, or may not, be actively involved with the planning of your trip. They may simply want you to present the itinerary and necessary forms to them for their approval or they may want to have monthly reports concerning the progress of trip preparations. You will need to find out specifically what they will want from you concerning the trip, and what the timeline will need to be for their approval.

The Leader would most likely report to the Board and would be responsible to them for the entire trip and for all those involved. In some cases there may be a Director, Coach or teacher who may, or may not, want to be the Leader also. Sometimes their responsibilities would be as such that they would not have the time to devote to arranging for a trip like this. They would much prefer to have someone else assume the responsibilities of the trip while they would have input and be a member of the Trip Committee. Good communication between everyone is imperative in a situation like this.

It is very important that the Leader is the **contact person** for all trouble shooting, and that they are the liaison to the parents and the Travel Agency. This is to insure that conflicting information is not given out before it is discussed with the Trip Committee and the Leader.

The Trip Committee responsibilities have already been outlined in preceding pages.

Once the trip begins the group of chaperones would report to the Leader or a "Head Chaperone" or an assistant as they have been instructed to do. Any instructors or other staff would need to be assigned someone to report to also, either the Director, Coach, etc. who would also report to the Leader.

Students and other trip members would report to their assigned chaperones on the trip. Parents and other involved persons would direct their questions to the Leader.

CHAPTER 2
-
"KICK OFF MEETING"

PLANNING YOUR "KICK OFF MEETING"

For an international trip for sure, and possibly for one in the United States, you will need to have a meeting for all those interested in going about 1 year before the actual trip is to take place. At this meeting you may present the preliminary itinerary, and the estimated total cost of the trip with a payment schedule, which would include the main payment covering the Travel Agency charges, and the expenses for things your group may be arranging (security, renting instruments, paperwork). Also, include an estimate of any additional expenses not covered by the Travel Agency and your group (extra meals, souvenirs) and an idea of costs of other items that will be needed for the trip: Passport, special clothes, luggage. Trip Commitment Forms should be handed out and requested to be returned that evening, or as soon as possible.

If your trip will be around Spring Break, typically the first week of April, you may be able to have this "Kick Off Meeting" around mid June of the year before. This could be after finals are over for the students, but before many of the families have left on vacation. This way those graduating seniors of that year won't feel so bad hearing about a trip they can't go on, and the students and chaperones going can begin to prepare for the trip. Also, if this is a high school group and you have incoming freshmen going on this trip, they will have more of a "high school" mindset if they are done with 8th grade.

This is the ideal of course. If you will need to make a payment to the Travel Agency before this time then you will need to have your meeting sooner.

The purpose of this meeting is to start informing students and parents about the upcoming trip. The meeting should give them some ideas of things they can do to prepare for the trip during the summer vacation and to enable them to be able to spread out some of the expenses.

You will want to make this meeting as informative as possible, as well as lots of fun. You want to be sure that everyone who would be interested in going on this trip knows about this meeting, especially the incoming new students for the next year, and all are encouraged to attend this meeting.

You will want to have copies available for all of: a preliminary itinerary, estimated costs and payment schedule, list of items that will be needed (Passport, special clothes and/or a clothing list, luggage, money belt, travel items), printed instructions on obtaining Passports, fundraising opportunities and/or scholarship information.

You will want to create a lot of excitement for the trip at this meeting and try to show that most all of them will be able to participate in this trip

2
"Kick Off Meeting"

if they start saving now, and take advantage of the fundraising opportunities and/or scholarships available.

The following is a suggested schedule to show students and parents how they can pay for this trip (suggested cost of $2000--$1500 basic cost, $500 to cover Passport, extra clothes, luggage, travel items, and spending money for meals and souvenirs) by budgeting $200 per month, starting in June for 10 months. Budgeting $300 per month for an adult or for a more generous budget is also shown.

10 Month Planning Budget

	Save	*Spend*
June	$200($300)	$80($100) for Passport, pictures
July	$200($300)	$60($150) for luggage, carry-on, daypack, toiletry bags
August	$200($300)	$20($30) for film (approx. 1 roll per day)
September	$200($300)	$200 for first payment
October	$200($300)	$300 for 2nd payment
November	$200($300)	$300 for 3rd payment
December	$200($300)	$40($70) for travel items (money belt, luggage tags, electrical converter)
January	$200($300)	$200 for 4th payment
February	$200($300)	$300 for 5th payment
March	$200($300)	$200 for 6th payment,remaining$300($1150) for meals/souvenirs/extra clothes

Hopefully this will help everyone to see that it is possible, with careful budgeting, to afford this trip. Of course, fundraisers and summer/after school jobs may impact this budget. Relatives may also help out with gifts of needed items and/or money also.

Another possibility might be a summer job where the student earns $1000 for the trip, the parent provides $500, fundraising and an after school job provides $500.

Please note that the $200/month is a very minimal budget. If more luggage, travel items, extra clothes are needed, more money will need to be budgeted. Also, if several meals will need to be paid for additional funds will be needed. The $300/month is much more generous and includes more money for meals, souvenirs and extra clothes.

The above budget does not include Trip/Travel Insurance, which will usually cost 5 to 8% of the total cost of the portion of the trip expenses covered by the Travel Agent. This amount will need to be considered in the budget if you will be purchasing Trip/Travel Insurance.

It will be helpful to your travelers if you are able to explain about the possibility of refunds to those who may have to cancel their trips. Usually without the purchase of Trip/Travel Insurance refunds will not be possible. Sometimes if the cancellation is early on, before any payments have been made to the Travel Agent some refund may be made. Also, your group may be able to refund a portion from the payments that are covering the expenses your group is providing, to a certain extent, but you probably won't be able to refund all of those either, especially the printing costs.

You will need to state what portion will not be refundable no matter what, maybe $50 or so, and then explain a timeline as to what will be refundable up to a certain time, and then what will be refundable with the purchase of Trip/Travel Insurance.

Travel Hints

You also want to build interest in the trip by giving some hints on luggage and travel items at this "Kick Off Meeting" in case families would like to purchase some of these items over the summer. Have some different types of suitcases, carry-ons and daypacks at the meeting, as well as an assortment of travel items: money belts, luggage tags, luggage locks (key and combination), toiletry bags, travel clocks, electricity converters).

Remind them of the dimensions allowed for carry-on bags (usually 22" X 14" X 8"), and that this **must** be adhered to. At a future meeting you might make up a box in these dimensions and have the students and adults bring their carry-ons to see if they will fit. This can be a lot of fun, and save a lot of hassle if they get to the airport and their carry-on doesn't fit in the airlines' "basket".

Also, explain how they may want to have a daypack for day tours, and to keep with them on plane flights. They can take this out of their carry-on to keep with them when they put the carry-on in the overhead bin.

Passport Photographs

Another thing you might want to do is to arrange to have a photographer at this meeting taking Passport photos. Sometimes a photographer will be willing to come to your meetings and take the Passport photos for a reduced price, since they will have several customers at once. Just be sure they have more than one person taking pictures if it is a large group, and that this takes place about 1 hour before the meeting is scheduled to begin, since you want everyone to attend this meeting on time. This will help people to get going on obtaining their Passports. You might want to repeat this at the October meeting for those who have not applied for their Passports by then.

Room Set Up and Commitment Forms

If you can find some posters about the countries and/or areas you will be visiting, you might want to mount them on tag board and have them on display during your meeting. A big map would be nice, too, possibly with the destinations and itinerary marked.

Just try to make this meeting fun, and informative, and reasonably short, 1.5 to 2 hours, and open to all those interested. You will also want to ask for a signed Commitment Form from the students and chaperones that want to go on the Trip. You could also have an area to check on the Commitment Forms if they would like to go but finances are a concern. This will give you an idea of the number of those wanting to go, and if this is close to the number you have been planning for. Also, you will be able to see how many may need scholarships.

The Commitment Forms will help you set up your trip data base and enable you to ascertain the number of students and chaperones going on the trip.

Action Plan For The Following Months:

- *Decide if you are going on this trip and fill out Commitment Form*
- *Begin setting aside money for the trip*
- *Begin looking for any needed luggage, travel items, clothes, film, and purchasing when desired*
- *Begin the process to obtain a Passport*

CHAPTER 3
-
GROUP MEETINGS

PLANNING YOUR LARGE GROUP MEETINGS

Even though summer is a time when people are gone a lot you still need to use this time to get prepared for the meetings coming up in the fall and winter. Since there will be a lot of paperwork that will need to be prepared, hopefully someone on the Trip Committee will volunteer to prepare the paperwork and get it printed. The Trip Committee can help collate and organize it. Speakers need to be sought out and booked for special presentations at your meetings. A calendar of meetings for those going on the trip needs to be compiled. It is very important to coordinate these meetings with the school calendar so there will not be a conflict. These Group meetings will need to be **mandatory** for those students and chaperones going on the trip, as well as at least one parent per family. This is really important because you need to know that all those concerned with the trip have heard the information presented.

Here is a suggested calendar starting in September for a trip taking place in April. You can adjust this to fit your trip schedule. It includes meeting topic suggestions and ideas for forms that need to be turned in.

Eight Month Calendar of Group Meetings

Month	*Topic*
September	Travel Agent: itinerary, costs, Travel Insurance

- *Turn in:* Trip Commitment Form

October	Passport instructions, picture ID, luggage, Rules and Guidelines

- *Turn in:* Trip Contract

November	Clothes, travel items, safety, first aid supplies

- *Turn in:* 2 copies of Picture Identification Card

December	Trip budget, finances, photography

- *Turn in:* 2 copies of Passport ID page

January	Carry-on items, health information

- *Turn in:* Field Trip Permission Form, Travel Agency Form, Special Power of Attorney (**notarized**)

February	Packing tips; "carry-on game"; sizes for shirts

- *Turn in* Medical Consent Form, Prescription drug list

March	Shopping tips, "money game"

- *Turn in:* Any remaining forms

April	Performance (optional, separate time) Last minute tips, student guidelines for behavior; Parent/chaperone discussion of assigned students

GROUP MEETING SUGGESTIONS

You will want to plan to have at least one large "Group" meeting a month, and one Committee meeting. Eventually, your Committee meeting may grow to include all the chaperones going on the trip too. It would probably be helpful to have the Committee meeting a week before the Group meeting, to aid in the organizing of the Group meeting. Also, you may want to meet with the Committee 1/2 hour before the Group meeting, and 1/2 hour afterwards, just to touch base with everyone, to hand out any paperwork, and for them to return to you the paperwork that has been turned in to them by the students.

Parents may tell you that they already know this stuff and don't see a need to attend another meeting. Traveling with students is different from traveling with a family. The Leader and the chaperones are assuming a huge responsibility in taking these students on this trip, so they need to expect that everyone is as prepared as possible to go on the trip and that the parents have heard the information presented too. Also, there will be some things that are unique to this trip and you want to be sure that there is clear communication among everyone involved. At least one parent from each family and all students, instructors and anyone else going on the trip need to be at each meeting.

Have the Trip Treasurer at each meeting to accept payments for the trip. He/she will need to come 1/2 hour early before the meeting starts to receive payments. He/she may want to collect payments after the meeting too. The Trip Treasurer will need to have his or her information as up to date as possible concerning any fundraising amounts that are available for students to use to make their payments too.

Small Groups

At the end of the meeting you will want the students to divide into small groups and hand in their "Trip Commitment" sheets if they haven't already. They will be handed the "Trip Contract" papers and the "Trip Folders" at this time. If the chaperone has written their names on them before they hand them out they will easily know if someone didn't come to their assigned group. Also, have the small group leader check off on the "Manila Envelope" if a student turns the Trip Commitment form in. (The details of this process will be covered later under "Paperwork".)

To facilitate this you will want to divide up all the students beforehand into groups of eight to ten and assign an adult to them. Arranging them alphabetically is the easiest way. Make an alphabetical list of all those students who have turned in Commitment Forms and divide them into groups. Do the same with the adults going on the trip.

You could use members of the Trip Committee as small group leaders for awhile and then add the chaperones later when you have assigned them students for the trip.

Pick out different areas in the room, and maybe rooms nearby, where everyone can have their small groups. A diagram of the meeting room(s) and the small group areas and names of group leaders on it can be handed out at the beginning of the meeting. Or you could assign numbers to each of the small groups and tape these (large) numbers up throughout your room(s). Read off the names in each group with their assigned number.

It will be helpful to meet with all the adult small group leaders before the main meeting to give them the envelopes to collect the items to be turned in and to give them any additional handouts that they need to give out.

Be sure to have some sort of attendance sheet in the small groups for the students and the parents with them to sign in on. These can be turned in at the meeting with the Leader after everyone has left. This will help you to easily know who was there and if any parents were missing. It is very important for parents to come to these meetings with their students. If attendance is taken they may be more likely to come.

There will need to be a person available to meet with any new people that want to come on the trip but haven't signed up yet. The leader of this small group can have copies of the Contracts and Trip Folders with them, and write the information of those new people on the labels on the Trip Folders. Be sure they make a list of those they gave Trip Folders to. Trip Commitment forms may be given to newcomers too, but ask them to hand those in that night.

After the adults are done meeting with their small groups have them meet together with the Leader to discuss the meeting and to return the manila envelopes. It would be helpful to have large rubber bands or clips to hold each group's envelopes together. If there is a separate check off sheet with the attendance and issues of concern they need to hand those in then.

The Leader will then need to look through the attendance sheets and other check off sheets to see how everyone is progressing with attendance and getting items turned in. He/she can then make note of any calls or contacts he/she will need to make with students and/or adults going on the trip to remind them of items they need to turn in or remind them that they need to attend the meetings.

You want to plan these meetings to move along quickly while being very informative. Try to have everything all set up at least 15 minutes to a half-hour before the meeting is scheduled to begin. If you are having a Committee meeting before the large Group meeting then you might need to have others help set up the room. Be sure to have any handouts that are going out to everyone set out in handy places for people to pick up. These would include the Agenda for the meeting and any notes and/or printed information. Other specific handouts may be handed out in the Small Groups. The following is a suggested agenda with a timetable.

Meeting Agenda Timetable

Time	*What*	*Who*
6:30-6:50	Committee Meeting	Leader, Committee, chaperones
7:00-7:05	Greeting, door prizes	Committee members
7:05-7:15	Update on Trip	Trip Leader
7:15-8:00	Presentation	Special Speaker, Committee members
8:00-8:15	Questions	Special Speaker, Leader
8:15-8:30	Turn in paperwork	Assigned Committee members
8:30-8:50	Committee Meeting	Leader, Committee, chaperones

It is very helpful to have a printed Agenda for each meeting. Be sure to leave room for people to take notes. Write the *Action Plan for the Next Month* at the bottom of the agenda. Have the date, time and place of the next meeting and when the next payment is due also written on the Agenda. You will need enough Agendas and copies of any notes that will be handed out for all the expected students, parents, and other adults attending the meeting, as well as a few extras. These can be given to anyone who could not make the meeting.

Be sure to save samples of all your trip paperwork for a file about the trip for people planning future trips for your group. Notes from your Trip Wrap-up Meeting should go in this file too.

Sample Large Group Meeting

6:30 *Committee Meeting*

- The Leader needs to meet with the Trip Committee and chaperones to briefly touch base with everyone and handout the Manila envelopes and other handouts to Small Group Leaders. If there are Trip Committee members who are not going on the trip they may be able to set up the room for the meeting: put up posters, table for presentations, hand out door prize tickets, agendas and any handouts to those arriving for the meeting.

7:00 *Greeting, Door Prizes*

- The meeting can be started with door prize drawings. This will help to get most everyone seated on time. Do the drawings while the late comers are finding their seats.

7:05 *Update on Trip*

- The Leader can then give any updates on the trip, discussing any changes to the itinerary. This is also a good time to point out locations you will be visiting on the trip on a large map. This helps orient people a little. It is also a good time to talk about some of the things everyone will be seeing on the trip, some of the history and culture. This will create excitement for the trip as well as providing some educational information.
- It would be nice to have descriptions of places and things you will be seeing in handouts to be given out at each meeting. They don't have to be very long. The Travel Agent may have information for you too. There is lots of information available on the Internet. Having posters with pictures of scenes from the countries you are visiting hung up on the walls, along with a large map can add a lot of "atmosphere" to your meeting room. You can mount these on tagboard for durability.

7:15 *Presentation, Special Speaker, Activity*

- At this time you would have your main informational presentation. This can be given by a special speaker, members of the Committee, the Leader of the trip. You could also have some sort of activity to involve the audience, such as guessing the cost of an item in a foreign currency and it's value in American money, a demonstration on packing a suitcase, showing items in a carry-on bag.

8:00 *Question and Answer Time*

- It's important to have a time for people to ask questions about the presentation and possibly the trip in general. Wrap up this part of the meeting by stating the suggested *Action Plans* for the following month.

8:15 *Small Groups, Turn in Paperwork*

- Everyone breaks into assigned small groups to check in for attendance, turn in any paperwork that is due and receive any additional handouts.
- You should plan to have some sort of paperwork turned in at every meeting so that there will be contact with each person going on the Trip with a Committee member. This helps to determine if each person was actually at this **mandatory** meeting and heard the information presented. If a student is sick or unable to attend the meeting they still need to have a parent attend and receive the information and turn in any paperwork that is due. The information you are presenting is very important and needs to be heard and taken seriously.

8:30 Committee Meeting

- Committee members and chaperones meet to touch base after the meeting, turn in the Manila envelopes and attendance sheets and discuss any concerns.

Sample of Printed Agenda

TRIP MEETING
October 8, 2002

Welcome and Door Prizes

Update on Trip

Presentation:
Passport information - Group Leader

Information about different types of luggage - Special Speaker

Questions

Small Groups
Turn in Trip Contract if haven't already

Action Plan For This Month:

- *Fill out Trip Contract to hand in at next month's meeting.*
- *Read through Trip Folder*
- *Have Passport pictures taken and apply for Passport if you haven't already*
- *Make 4 copies of your Picture Identification Card*
- *Get out the luggage you plan on taking and check them and/or buy new luggage as needed*

Calendar
October 10, Payment due, $300
November 12, Tuesday, next Trip Meeting, 7:00 PM
Turn in: Trip Contract; 2 copies of Picture Identification Card

FIRST MEETING IN SEPTEMBER WITH TRAVEL AGENT

Your first meeting in September may have to deviate some from this plan if you have the Travel Agent speak to your group. The agent will need enough time to explain many aspects of the Trip, including the itinerary, how many meals are provided, how much money is needed for meals and snacks that are not provided, types of clothes needed, trip insurance, and to answer any other questions. This may take longer that the allotted 45 minutes, but it is important that everyone's questions are answered. Trip/Travel insurance application forms will need to be dealt with also.

Since your Committee has been meeting with the Travel Agent a few times already you may be able to print up some of the information and have it available to hand out at the meeting. Hopefully your Agent is experienced in speaking before large groups, including many students. If not, possibly your Leader may want to give them a few pointers in speaking to them, such as treating them just like adults, not talking down to them, and keeping the meeting moving.

Another thing to do that a traveling group I know has done is have your Trip Committee meeting discuss specific questions that you want answered by the Travel Agent in front of the large group. Then divide those questions up among the members of the Trip Committee. They will then see that those questions get asked in the large group meeting. Preparing ahead like this is very helpful because once you are in the meeting it is sometimes easy to get distracted or sidetracked by other issues and not really get the necessary and practical questions answered.

At this meeting you may want to get a signed Commitment Form from each person who wants to go on the trip if they haven't turned one in already. This will give you a more accurate number of those students going, as well as the number of chaperones. Hopefully this number will be really close to what you have planned for. You can hand the forms out at the beginning of the meeting and ask them to turn them in to their Small Group Leader.

If you are planning on giving out some scholarships you will need to have those applications printed up and handed out as soon as you can. Be sure to give the date to have them returned and to whom. The recipients will need to be determined some time before the first payment is due, since this may be a determining factor if they are able to go on the trip or not.

Be sure to explain to the Group what items the Travel Agency is arranging and what items that your Committee is handling and possibly other additional costs if you know them at this time.

PAYMENTS

You will need to determine a payment schedule that will meet your needs as well as fit the payment schedule that the Travel Agency has set for you. Typically they may need 2 or 3 payments from you to first secure the airline seats, and then to secure the "land package" of lodging, meals, entrances into attractions and transportation. You may want to spread out payments to make it easier on your families, and to give you flexibility in the items you will be arranging for in addition to what the Travel Agency is doing. You will need to know at what point the payments will be nonrefundable and/or nontransferable.

Sometimes, usually before the airline tickets are purchased, you may be able to add additional people to those going on the trip, and/or add people if someone drops out. There will be a point, however, when this will not be possible. If someone cannot go on the trip after this point, Trip Cancellation Insurance may help somewhat, if they have bought it and have to cancel because of illness, family emergency, or some other specified reason.

It's important that you decide how much, and at what point you will refund any payments that are made, since you will be incurring expenses in addition to the payments to the Travel Agency.

A suggested schedule of payments would be:

1st Payment	September 10	$200
2nd Payment	October 10	$300
3rd Payment	November 10	$300
4th Payment	January 10	$200
5th Payment	February 10	$300
6th Payment	March 1	$200

It will be really nice for your group if you can wait until September to start collecting payments. It just seems that most groups have more of a "trip mindset" at the beginning of the school year. However, there may be a lot of expenses for your parents in August and September for the beginning of a school year, so you will need to discuss this with your Committee. A lot will depend upon when your first payment is due to the Travel Agency.

Another thing to consider is that you want to have a pretty good idea of how many people actually plan on going on the trip. Having to put money down on a trip helps people to make that commitment. You also may need some money to pay for the printing costs, door prizes, during the summer. So you may want to have some sort of refundable payment due in June, maybe $50 to $100. Then you could reduce the September payment to $100 or so.

Do remember that the Travel Agency may want to have any Trip/Travel Insurance paid for at the meeting when they present the information or within a few days afterward. Since this amount could be around $100 or so you may want to prepare your travelers for this beforehand. If you can obtain the information on Trip/Travel Insurance before hand you may want to give this information to your travelers so that they have time to read it over before the meeting with the Travel Agent.

The final payment may need to be earlier in the month than the other payments have been if the Travel Agency needs all the money a month before the trip. These payments would be made to your group. The actual Travel Agency payments would be due on different dates and may only be three or four actual payments. You will need time to document all the payments, deposit the money and forward the payments to the Travel Agency. Be sure to allow yourself enough time to handle all these details between payments that are due to the Travel Agency.

The Committee will need to determine how these payments are to be handled. If the trip is a school sponsored one you may have to give all the payments to the school treasurer and then they would make the payments to the Travel Agency and for all the other bills. However, your school may not want to be bothered with any of this so your organization (booster group or a similar group) may need to run everything through it's treasury.

In any case you will need to set up a system for accepting payments, unless your school sends a representative to accept payments. You may want the Treasurer to set up a table at each large group meeting and accept payments there. You might also want the Treasurer to receive payments through the mail.

If your organization is handling fundraising opportunities you will have to determine how this money is allocated to the students. You will need to decide on some type of form that is used so you can keep track of the payments and any money that is used from fundraising opportunities.

For example, with our Band Booster Organization we offered fund raising opportunities to the students. After expenses, the money left was split 20% for the Boosters and 80% for each student's account according to how much they had worked on that particular fundraiser. The money in the student's account could only be spent on approved Booster items, the main one being Band Trips.

To withdraw money from the student's account a parent needed to sign a form to allow the Booster Treasurer to spend the money toward approved items. Cash could not be withdrawn from the account!

I would suggest that you have payment forms in the Trip Folder as well as available at every meeting. Have the Treasurer's name, address and phone number clearly stated on the form so they can mail a payment if they want to. This really helps avoid long lines of travelers waiting to give payments to the Treasurer on the nights of your Group meetings.

Have the date, payment method: check #, amount withdrawn from student account, and total amount paid, plus a signature line for the parent, as well as a line for the student or chaperone's name. This form needs to be turned in with **each** payment and the Treasurer needs to keep these in case of a disagreement later over payments. Have some form of receipt to be handed back with this information on it too. Possibly the Treasurer could give the receipt to the "small group" leaders to hand back to the students from those who mailed in payments. There could be a sheet in the Trip Folder with a list of the payment due dates and a place to indicate the date that payment was paid, the check # and any amount that was used from a student's fundraising "account". Perhaps the treasurer could initial that form instead of having separate receipts for each payment.

You can decide if you want students and chaperones payments on the same form if they are from the same family and pay with the same check. They are listed that way on the following sample form.

The Treasurer will need to keep an up do date accounting of all payments paid as well as having amounts available in student accounts. This can be rather tricky but it can be done. One group I know of sent out accounting statements every month with the Group's newsletter. There was a payment form included so they could make a payment after they received the statement and knew how much was in their student account. This is a big job so be sure to help out your Treasurer as much as possible.

This also means that any fundraising chairmen need to get in the results of the fundraiser as soon as possible. They will need to show the amount that each person earned in the fundraiser so the Treasurer can then credit the amount to that person's account. If there are several fundraisers very careful records need to be kept and fundraising chairmen need to be encouraged to get the information in as quickly as possible.

Sample Trip Payment Form

( ) TRIP PAYMENT

Date______________

Student Name:____

$_____________Check Check # __________

$_____________Deducted from Student Account (Parent's Signature required)

$_____________**Total Paid**

Parent's Signature______________________________

Chaperone Name:____

$____________Check Check # __________

Please make checks payable to: Band Boosters

Please note there will be a $25.00 returned check charge.

Payments may be given to the Booster Treasurer in person or mailed to:

Booster Treasurer
Band Boosters
1234 Highland
Everett, WA 98208

One important thing to consider concerning payments is the use of credit cards. Most schools and booster groups for that matter, are not set up to accept credit card payments. Most Travel Agencies will accept credit card payments. There are certain advantages for travelers when paying for their flights with a credit card. Many credit card companies will offer flight insurance and/or lost luggage insurance when the "trip" is charged. However, credit card companies may differ widely on what is provided and what portion of the trip needs to be charged on the card.

You may want to discuss this with your Travel Agent and see if it is possible to charge a certain portion, or even the entire amount that they are providing for each individual person. Any additional things that your group is providing: transportation to and from your "home" airport, paperwork costs, transporting instruments or special shirts would be a separate payment just to your group. This may become too complicated with a large group, or your Travel Agent may have a system worked out for these situations already.

This can work very well for your travelers, allowing them to spread the payments out over a longer period of time, though possibly with interest charges.

However, it may be difficult to implement this if your group is doing a lot of fundraising and students have their own fundraising accounts. Usually a nonprofit group will not want to write checks back to individuals from their fundraising "accounts". The group will want to write one large check to the Travel Agency. Students would not be able to use money from their fundraising accounts to pay the credit card charge.

You will want to thoroughly discuss this situation with your Travel Agency and your Committee before you have any payments due. Parents will probably ask you questions about this issue so be prepared.

PAPERWORK

To make this trip as organized as possible, all along the way, and to keep everyone (parents and students) informed and educated, will involve quite a bit of paperwork. To begin with, even 1 1/2 years before the trip will take place, you will want to be sending out informational flyers to all those who may be interested in going on the trip, including preliminary itineraries and cost estimates. Once you begin group meetings there will be a lot of additional printing and paperwork costs for handouts, notes, forms.

You will need to decide who will cover the printing costs of all of these. If your trip is a school sponsored one, the school itself may be willing to cover these costs. However, some schools are so strapped for money that this may be a cost they are unwilling or unable to bear. You may want to charge each person going on the trip an additional $5 to $10 to cover the paperwork costs. This is a reasonable thing to charge, and should not be overlooked, since these costs can add up significantly.

It would be very helpful if the Trip Committee would be able to prepare a lot of these items before the meetings, possibly over the summertime.

For the items that must be filled out and returned it is probably best to have them handed out when they meet with the small group leader at the end of the meeting during the Small Group time. The person's name should be written on the item and then handed out individually. This way you know that each person has received the item. Just having them in a pile at the door is not very helpful, and can cause a lot of irritation for those who claim they never received the information. You will also know if that person wasn't there, or didn't bother to pick up the item.

In the preliminary planning for the trip you may need to mail certain items out to all those you think might be interested in going on the trip. Items could include preliminary itineraries, meeting and payment schedules, Commitment Forms. This way you will know that all the families received the information.

Communication is key in a trip like this, involving so many students, chaperones and parents. Information needs to be **heard, seen** and **read** to really be effective, and remembered.

Envelopes

As the trip begins to come together, and you begin getting Commitment Forms from those going on the trip you will need a system to organize these, and the additional papers that you will need to get from each person during the months ahead. I would suggest that you prepare a large Manila Envelope for each person going on the trip. On the outside affix a label with the name, (parent's name also, if student) address and phone number of each person. Also, staple a sheet of paper with a check list of the items that you will need to gather from each person: Trip Contract, 2 copies of Passport information page, 2 copies of Picture Identification Card, Field Trip Permission Form, Medical History Information and Consent to Treat form, Special Power of Attorney and any other needed forms on the outside of the envelope.

At each meeting ask to have one of these items due. Have your Committee members or chaperones check off the items as they come in. They can then tell the Leader who has not turned in their items. This saves the Leader from having to check every person's information at each meeting. Maybe you can have a single attendance sheet for each Committee member/chaperone to fill out, stating those students and parents present, whoever did not hand in the required paperwork, and any other pertinent information. A suggested copy is in the Appendix.

It is really important to have deadlines when certain forms, copies of the Passport and Picture Identification and other paperwork are due. Many of these items are **mandatory** for everyone to fill out and turn in if they are going on the trip. You don't want everyone to wait until the last minute to turn these in. You also want to know that everyone has obtained a Passport and have a Picture Identification Card. With the deadlines and check list you can easily see if everyone has filled out and turned in the required paperwork. This will relieve a lot of the stress on the travelers as well as help you tremendously in the organization of all the paperwork.

Travel Folder

Another helpful item is a Travel Folder for each person going on the trip, as well as one for each family. These would contain copies of the signed Contract, calendar of meetings and payment due dates, itinerary, handouts from meetings, budget for trip and payment forms. Labels with the family name on one and another one with the name, address and phone number for each of the students and chaperones going on the trip. This will be helpful if they are misplaced. You may set a replacement fee for these Folders if they are lost, since each person needs to bring the Folder to every meeting and may need to take this Folder on the trip as well. Be sure to make up several extras just in case.

These Folders can be simple "pee chee" type with pockets, and possibly 3 ring fasteners inside for keeping much of the paperwork in order.

TRIP DATA BASE

When you begin to get the Trip Commitment Forms back you will want to put the information into a computer database. This will help you a great deal later when you need lists of those going on the trip. You will want to have line items for name, address, phone number, if they are a student or adult/chaperone, the name of the student's parent/legal guardian, and the name of the chaperone's student. An area to write in the student's assigned chaperone would be helpful later for lists of chaperone groups.

This way you can make mailing labels, envelope labels, lists of students, lists of chaperones, and other lists very easily. You will need to give some of this information to the Travel Agency too so this will help facilitate this. The Leader would be the logical one to create this database and to keep it updated. However, it could be delegated to someone else on the Committee to handle if need be.

FORMS

While having so many forms to fill out for a trip may seem like a lot of work, and maybe not really necessary, it really does help the trip preparation go a lot easier for everyone involved. Some of the forms are **absolutely necessary** for the Leader and chaperones to have when they are responsible for someone else's children on a trip in the United States and especially in other countries. Most will never need to be used, but if something happens it will be vital to have this information.

The forms provided are only suggestions for the Leader and Committee to look at and change as needed. If you have any questions about legality or liability you may want to consult with an attorney about the forms you should use. For a school sponsored trip the School District may have their own forms that you will need to use.

The following is a list of suggested forms to use and explanations of why they are needed. The actual forms are found in the Appendix at the end of the book.

**Trip Commitment Form* - Gives the Leader an idea of who is going on the trip and provides basic information for trip data base: name, address, phone number, student, adult, chaperone.

**Trip Contract* - Student and Parent sign this committing to go on the trip, make the payments on time and to follow the Rules and Guidelines.

Travel Agency Information - Contains information that the Travel Agency will probably need

**Authorization Form for Administration of Medication* - Parent signs this to indicate that they have given their student permission to take the listed prescription and over-the-counter medication.

**Medical History and Consent to Treat Form* - Contains vital medical history information, insurance information and gives medical authorities permission to treat medical situations.

Special Power of Attorney* - Gives Leader and chaperones permission to take students on the trip and allows them to act in the best interests of the students in situations where the parents of the students are not available. **This form must be signed by the parents and notarized.

Trip Payment Record - Easy way to keep track of payments being made for the trip

Attendance Sheet - Record of students & parents attendance at meetings

Calendar of Items to be turned in - Reminds everyone when meetings are and what items need to be turned in at each one.

Field Trip Permission Form - Sample of the type of form a School District may need each student and parent to fill out for a school sponsored trip.

Departure Day Check List - Suggested list of items that chaperones will need to check off with their assigned students on departure day.

*These forms and information are **absolutely necessary** for most trips you will take students and/or anyone else on.

The other information and forms may or may not be needed for your trip but may be very helpful.

FUN STUFF

There are many things that you can do to make your meetings and your trip more fun. A few members of your Committee may enjoy putting together some of the following things. If they are too busy, you may want to ask some others from your group to help out gathering and arranging the items.

Door Prizes

One fun thing we did at our meetings was to have door prizes. We had separate baskets of prizes for students and adults. We handed out tickets as people came into the meetings and usually gave out 3 or 4 prizes for each group at each meeting. Adults will really like being included too.

You can have many different prizes: possibly getting them donated, or just making them a budgeted item. Prizes can range from candy bars to travel items (money belts, luggage locks and tags, sewing kits, travel size toiletries), and everything in between. They don't have to be expensive. A candy bar goes over great. Boxes of various sizes of ziplock bags are great too. Just have a basket full of items and let the winners choose what they want. This will make your meetings more fun, and are a great way to get people there on time. Just have your drawings at the beginning of the meeting. People love winning things so they will even get there early!!!

You may be able to get different stores to donate some of these items. Maybe a drug store would let you choose 10 or so items from their bins of trial sized items. Just stress that it is for students.

"Trip Survival Kits"

The Trip Committee I was on for the England trip made up "Trip Survival Kits" for the students, chaperones and instructors. We were able to get a lot of the items donated from various businesses so this kept the costs down considerably. I would suggest that you mention them to your large group, and possibly put an article in your newsletter if you have one. You may find parents in your group that have businesses that may be able to donate items. There may be groups your students are involved with that may be willing to donate. These could be local businesses: music stores, hotels, dentists, travel agents or maybe special interest groups: Army, Navy, U. S. Customs, local police, "Dare" Program, who have special imprinted items to advertise their group.

Most of the items listed were in the "Survival Kits" we made up for the England Trip but I have added some additional items that would be nice to have. Hopefully you will be able to get most of the items donated.

Examples:

Donated items

Luggage tags: local music store with their name imprinted on
Pens: with business name imprinted on
Toothpaste and dental floss: local dentist
Small bars of soap: local hotel where we held our annual auction
Note pads: local business
Key chains: local business, special group
Water bottles: local business, special group
Sewing kits: local business, special group

Purchased items

Ziplock bags: Sandwich, Quart & Gallon size
- Student "Kits" were put in quart size
- Chaperone "Kits" were put in gallon size
- Quart size we put label on with "Receipts" written on
  - *So everyone could have a bag for their receipts
- Sandwich size held 2-3 small bars of soaps

Chewing gum
Hard candy individually wrapped, lifesavers
Band-Aids
Handiwipes
Safety pins
Yarn pieces to mark suitcases

Chaperones and instructors received more band-aids, safety pins, and handiwipes, as well as mouthwash and larger toothpastes in their "Survival Kits."

We had a meeting to put the "Kits" together and then handed them out to thc students and chaperones. We even made some up for the six instructors and the Band Director and his wife. They were all very thrilled to get them.

I suggest that you hand these out at the January meeting. This will help your travelers in their planning of items they may need to buy. These items are all very useful items that most everyone will need. Be sure to make sure everyone receives one. You might want to hand them out during the small group meetings and in the meeting with the chaperones and other adults going on the trip.

CHAPTER 4

-

MONTHLY MEETINGS

MONTHLY MEETING SUGGESTIONS AND ACTION PLANS

The following are suggestions for the information to be given out at the monthly large group meetings. There are also suggested "Action Plans" of things for those going on the trip to do during the weeks until the next large group meeting. Spreading out the many things that need to be done in preparing for a trip over several months helps everyone not to feel so pressured and rushed the last few weeks before departure. It also helps distribute the expenses over several months' time rather than bunching them up to the last few weeks before you leave on the trip. Additional information for these topics are found in Part Two.

SEPTEMBER MEETING: TRAVEL INSURANCE

This meeting will be primarily with the Travel Agent and that person will be explaining the itinerary, describing the countries and sights they will be seeing, estimated expenses covered by the trip payment and those things not covered (meals, souvenirs, Travel Insurance, etc). There will need to be plenty of time for questions. The Agent needs to explain Travel Insurance very carefully, and answer the questions as completely as possible. Application forms for Travel Insurance need to be handed out too. This is an area that needs to be dealt with very carefully because there is a potential for much misunderstanding and anger if people have to cancel their trip, or have a medical emergency while on the trip, and have not purchased Travel Insurance, and then claim they were not properly informed.

Parents need to check to see if their medical insurance will cover them while overseas. Most will, but will reimburse when you get back. So you will have to pay the expenses over there first. Medicare does not cover you out of the United States. Sometimes a school may be able to offer low cost medical insurance plans for students. Be sure to check on this.

There may be two separate types of Travel Insurance offered, or they may be bundled together. One would cover the trip costs that are provided by the Travel Agent. Buying this type of Trip Cancellation Insurance would provide a certain amount of refundablity of the payments made for the trip if a traveler became ill before the trip departure date and was unable to participate. Also, if a close family member became ill and the traveler needed to stay home. Other instances may be provided for also.

Medical Insurance and Trip Evacuation Insurance usually cover a traveler while traveling in a foreign country. The traveler's medical expenses are then covered and if medical evacuation is needed, it is provided for. Other services may be provided for also. The policy needs to be read very carefully and thoughtfully before a decision is made.

The Travel Agent may want to discuss "Frequent Flyer Miles" at this time also. The Agent should be able to tell you what airlines you will be using and how to apply for Frequent Flyer Miles. Usually you will need to be signed up with the airline and have received a member number. You will need to give this number to the Agent. Sometimes different airlines have reciprocal agreements and will honor another airlines' miles. Your Agent should be able to give you information on this.

Trip Commitment forms should be turned in at this meeting if they haven't been turned in already. You may want to hand out copies of the Trip Contract at this time and have the trip leader explain what it means: a contract to go on the trip, to make the payments on time, and to agree to follow the behavior requirements as stated.

Action Plan for This Month:

- *Fill out Commitment Forms and Trip Contract if available*
- *Check with medical insurance company and decide on purchase of Trip/Travel Insurance*
- *Read over Rules and Guidelines for Trip*

OCTOBER MEETING: TRAVEL DOCUMENTS, LUGGAGE

During this meeting you will want to explain to everyone how to obtain Passports and Picture Identification Cards, if they do not have driver's licenses. If most of the people do not have their Passports yet you might want to have a Passport photographer at your meeting again, an hour before it begins to take Passport pictures. This would also be a good time to have someone describe the different types of luggage available, and their pros and cons. You might be able to have someone from a specialty luggage store to do this because they should be very knowledgeable. However, they may also want to sell you expensive luggage too.

Small Groups in Action

At this meeting you will hope to have firm commitments from most everyone who wants to go on this trip. You will want to have the Trip Folders and the manila envelopes made up for each person going on the trip. Have a brief meeting with the Committee/chaperones to hand out the manila envelopes. The simplest way to organize these envelopes is to alphabetize them, adults and students separately. Then divide the students up into groups of 8 or so, depending upon the number of adults available. At first you may want to just use Committee members, although some of these may be chaperones too, until you get to know the chaperones better.

Or you may want to start all the chaperones off helping with this. Later on you will want to reorganize the small groups into the assigned chaperone groups they will be in on the Trip, and have the chaperone assigned to each group help collect the information from their own group.

You may want to post a list of names for each adult up on a wall, and indicate where in the room they will be when it is time to check in with their small group. Discuss this with the adults involved, and decide on locations for each group. You may need to read off the names and locations to everyone. Don't forget to have someone available to meet with those who may not be on your lists but now want to go on the trip.

You will probably hand out the Trip Contract at this time if you have not already done so, and ask to have the Contract returned at the November Meeting. The signed Trip Commitment Form should be in the Manila Envelope already, or put in it at this meeting. You will need to have a copy of the Rules and Guidelines available for each family and you will want to go over it briefly, emphasizing the Rules and Consequences.

Depending upon the number of Small Group Leaders that you have you will want to have a "Head Group Leader" and maybe an assistant, and divide up the adult traveler Envelopes among them, alphabetically. This will help things go more quickly if you only have 8 or so assigned to either the "Head" or the assistant. The Small Group Leaders who are adult travelers then turn in their paperwork to the "Head" the same way you are asking the students to, with another check off sheet filled out by the "Head". Usually do this part <u>before</u> the meeting, so that it is "training" in what they will be doing with the students. Also, hand out the adult and student information to the Small Group Leaders. These forms will need to be returned and/or kept in each participant's Trip Folder. The Small Group Leaders can write the students' names on the handouts so they will be sure they have handed them out to each one. If attendance sheets are being used these will need to be given to the Small Group Leaders too.

If you are having a speaker you may have additional notes that may be available as people come in the door. Remind everyone to pick them up at the opening of the meeting, along with the Agenda for the meeting.

There may be a lot of questions from the parents at this meeting, so you may want to allow extra time for this. You will also want to talk some about the itinerary and about some of the wonderful sights that you are going to see. Try to create some excitement about the trip.

If you think there might be enough time in the meeting you might want to bring in an outside speaker, possibly from a country that you may be visiting, to give them some insight into the language and the culture. It is always nice to hear another's perspective.

Action Plan For This Month:

- *Fill out Trip Contract to hand in at next month's meeting.*
- *Read through Trip Folder*
- *Have Passport pictures taken and apply for Passport if you haven't already*
- *Make 4 copies of your Picture Identification Card*
- *Get out the luggage you plan on taking and check them and/or buy new luggage as needed*

NOVEMBER MEETING: TRAVEL ITEMS AND CLOTHING

This meeting should center about very specific travel items that those going on the trip need to be thinking about, purchasing, or putting on their Christmas lists. There should also be a discussion on clothing for the trip. If there are specific expectations about the types of clothing to be worn these need to be explained very clearly to everyone involved, even written down and handed out to all so there are no misunderstandings at the airport or thousands of miles away. This should be done now so that everyone has enough time to purchase any items they need and spread the costs over several months. They might receive some things for Christmas or birthday gifts. Don't forget to talk about performance clothes if they are needed.

It is also helpful as far as expenses go to begin gathering travel size toiletry and cosmetic items as well as first aid supplies.

Action Plan For This Month:

- *Buy the travel items you will need, or make a Christmas List and tell those who might want to buy them for you*
- *"Trial Pack" the clothes and other items you think you want to take on the trip*
- *List what new clothes and items that you are going to need to purchase or hopefully receive as gifts*
- *Begin gathering travel size toiletry items*
- *Begin gathering first aid supplies*

DECEMBER MEETING: TRIP FINANCES, PHOTOGRAPHY

At this meeting I would encourage you to have the Group Leader begin with information on a "Trip Budget", finances and foreign money. Also discuss how the group will handle financial emergencies that occur on the trip. Then I would suggest that you try to find a speaker who can present simple suggestions on cameras and taking pictures. If you can't find anyone then have a Committee Member or the Group Leader present the information presented in the chapter on photography, plus additional tips from the Group. I am not an expert on photography, but have provided practical information.

Action Plan For This Month:

- *Try to determine a realistic spending budget for meals, snacks and souvenirs*
- *Families discuss use of cash, ATM cards and credit cards and arrange for obtaining them if needed*
- *Obtain a camera and film if you haven't already, or put it on your Christmas list*
- *Practice with your camera so you know how all the features work*

JANUARY MEETING: HEALTH, CARRY-ONS, ROOMMATES

At this meeting you would discuss the Medical History, Medical Release and Consent to Treat Form. Be sure to emphasize any forms that need to be returned and who needs to sign them. Sometimes a form needs a doctor's signature. Parents need to start getting these forms ready.

Whoever will be going as the trip "nurse/medical person" should also address the group as to all the travelers' health for the trip and some things they can do to help take care of themselves and to feel good on the trip. Hints to help them to prepare for the trip as well as during the trip: getting enough rest, drinking enough water. There should also be an explanation as to what students are to do if they do become sick: telling their chaperone and the "nurse/medical person" and not trying to hide it.

Parents also need to be encouraged to talk with their students about taking care of themselves, explaining what over-the-counter medications they will be carrying and when to take them.

Also, the policy on carrying prescription drugs and over-the-counter drugs needs to be explained to the parents. The need for a form listing all the prescription drugs and over-the-counter drugs that each person is carrying should be explained too.

This is also a time to explain about luggage, specifically about "Carry-on" bags: what needs to go in them and what items they need to pack in their large suitcase. You can have a few different types of bags there and show the items in them. Have a "box" in the allowed dimensions for them to see what the size needs to be. For the next meeting ask everyone to bring his or her carry-on bags to the meeting. They can "trial fit" them in the box to make sure they will fit. You might want to have a little game of going through a list of the items you talked about at this meeting and see how many have packed them in their bag. Have everyone stand up then sit down when they don't have an item you mention. The last one standing gets a prize. This helps everyone to gain ideas about what others are bringing and what things they may, or may not, want to bring.

If your group is making up the "Survival Kits" that were mentioned before, this meeting might be a good time to hand these out. The reason for this is that some of the items you might have included in the "Survival Kits" may be things that your travelers may be starting to obtain now.

Another thing you need to do at this meeting is talk about roommate assignments. This is an area where you need to be very sensitive to the students you are working with. Most of them will have natural friends that they will want to room with. The trick is getting them assigned to their preferred roommates. There will also be "loners" who don't seem to have many friends so will have a tough time choosing roommates.

You will want to discuss with the students that you will honor their choices as much as possible but may need to make some adjustments. They will need to understand that there may be some combinations of friends that may not be a very good idea and that as the Leader of the group you may need to modify roommate requests. Also, once they make their roommate requests and the roommate list has been decided they will not be able to change them except for emergencies. They need to choose carefully and live with their choice.

I suggest that you put up a sign-up sheet in the meeting room. Hopefully you will have a room where this sign-up sheet can stay up for a few weeks so students will have time to think about their requests and sign up. If you do not have a place for this you will need them to turn their requests in at the meeting or mail them to you. Be sure to give them a deadline.

Decide what is the smallest number of roommates for your housing sites, as well as the most common number. If you are staying in the same housing site the whole time this will be very easy. You may be in a hotel the whole time with rooms of four for all students.

However, you may have a mixture of room assignments at different housing sites. On the England trip I was on we had two, four, six and more as well as single rooms in a university dorm on several different nights.

If you have mostly rooms of four housing sites, with some rooms of two at other housing sites I would suggest the following sign-up form:

Roommate Requests

Girls	Boys
Room # 1	Room # 1
________________	________________
________________	________________
________________	________________
________________	________________
Room # 2	Room # 2
________________	________________
________________	________________
________________	________________
________________	________________
Room # 3	Room # 3
________________	________________
________________	________________
________________	________________
________________	________________

etc. etc. etc.

There may be an odd number of students so you will have to have rooms of three sometimes. If you see this before you have the sign-up you may tell the students there will be a room of three boys/girls and they can sign up for this if they want.

After the sign-up form has been up for awhile you will want to check off those signed up against your master list of students. You can then talk to those who haven't signed up yet to encourage them to sign up and suggest who still needs a roommate. Tell them if they do not sign up by a certain date you will assign them roommates.

Once you have "closed" the roommate assignments you will want to make chaperone assignments. You will want to discuss with your chaperones if they have any special requests about which students they would like to chaperone. They may want to chaperone their own children or they may have a friend who wants them to chaperone their children. Also, if there are any special needs students that need a certain chaperone you will have to consider that.

Chaperones do not necessarily have to chaperone their own children though sometimes they will want to. Sometimes the students don't want their parents to chaperone them. This is something you may have to deal with so you will want open communication with all of them.

First you will need to determine how many students you will need to put with each chaperone. You may be limited by the number of chaperones you have with the number of students. Also, you may have more female chaperones than male, but more male students. Then you will have to assign some female chaperones to some of the male students. Sometimes the male student's moms will want to chaperone their sons. Also, you may need to assign more students to certain chaperones simply because you have more student groups than chaperones and you want to keep the roommates together in the chaperone groups. You may see that some of the roommate groups may be more difficult to chaperone than others and you may want to choose specific chaperones for those students that you feel will be able to better handle that particular group. Room assignments seem to work best for this so that the chaperones can check on their assigned students easily at bed check time. Four to eight students per chaperone usually works really well, with four being ideal.

I would suggest that you show your chaperones the roommate assignments of the students and ask for their input. Discuss with them any situations that you may have where you want certain students to have certain chaperones. Chaperones can then suggest which student roommate groups that they would prefer to chaperone. If they don't really know some of the students you may have to assign them or let them choose their groups.

Then it is best to post the roommate lists with the assigned chaperones. This helps the students know who their chaperones are. Hopefully, you won't have any complaints.

The Leader of the group and the "Trip Nurse/medical person" should not be assigned any students to chaperone. They will be busy enough and need to be free of the responsibilities of chaperoning. If you have enough chaperones to allow for possibly others to do specific jobs and not chaperone this can be very helpful too. What I am thinking of here is possibly an "Equipment Manager" and maybe a helper or two, who would be in charge of the instruments if you have them. Sometimes it is hard to do this job and chaperone because the person(s) will be busy packing up the instruments, when they may be needed to chaperone. Students may choose those times to push the limits when they know their chaperone is distracted and busy. However, this all depends upon the amount of chaperones and students that you have. Students will probably be helping with the instruments too, but there still needs to be an adult in charge of this area.

Don't forget to discuss with your chaperones as to their own roommate requests. **Don't assume anything!** Be sure to discuss any special circumstances when you might have adults in with a group of students.

You want to have this all done by the February meeting so that the parents can meet their students' assigned chaperones and get to know them. At this meeting you will want to change the Small Groups to the chaperone groups and have the students turn in their paperwork to their chaperone. The medical forms will be turned in at this meeting so the parents can discuss any health concerns with the chaperone and the nurse.

Action Plan For This Month

- *Fill out Medical Information and Medical Release and Consent to Treat Form; have signed by parents and doctor, if needed*
- *Turn in notarized Special Power of Attorney*
- *Gather items for Carry-on bag*
- *Pack Carry-on bag and bring to next meeting*
- *Students sign up roommate requests*
- *Chaperones choose student groups to chaperone*

FEBRUARY MEETING: PACKING, CARRY-ON GAME

This meeting could be a time for packing discussion and tips. Also, you could have a "carry-on game" to illustrate some of these tips. Ask everyone to bring his or her carry-on bags, fully packed, to this meeting. Tell them to come a half-hour or so early so everyone will have time to measure and weigh their bags. Have a "box" in the dimensions that the airlines will allow for carry-ons, as well as a scale to weigh the bags with. For those wanting to participate in the game ask them to check their bags in the "box" first, and weigh them. If their bags don't fit, or weigh too much they can't "play". Some may not want to "play" so you may want to ask them to measure and check their bags later if you are running out of time.

Begin the game by asking all to stand who have measured and weighed their bags and their bags meet the standards. Start listing the items they need to have in their carry-on: luggage tag, identifying mark, name and address inside bag, full change of clothes, First Aid items (band-aids, pain reliever minimum), toiletries, tissues, lip balm, sunglasses, camera, trip folder, something else to read, pen or pencil and paper, something to keep occupied (cards, games) snacks, bottle of water, gum.

If someone doesn't have one of these items as they are called off they sit down. Keep adding items from the list in this book if most of them have these items, though remember that some of the items will be specific to the person: prescription drugs, contact supplies and glasses, women's supplies. Hopefully you will come up with one winner, though you may end up with many. You can decide if you want to give out prizes.

This game helps everyone to see what types of bags others are taking and what kinds of things they have. It helps everyone to think about what they are taking and what they may have forgotten, or if they are taking too many things.

After the game you can bring out a large suitcase and give some packing tips on how to pack. It would be nice to have all the items needed for the average person for the trip available so you show how to fit them all into the suitcase. Show how to use the different sizes of ziplock bags to hold different items too.

If you are having special shirts made for everyone you will need to get all of the sizes of those going on the trip. You might want to have sample shirts for everyone to try on to check for the correct size. Have some sort of form for everyone to fill out with room for their name and size on it. Order the shirts as soon as possible so they will be ready in time for your trip.

These shirts can be many different styles and colors, depending upon what use you want them for. You may want them simply as a commemorative item they would only wear once or twice on the trip. Or they could be used as a type of "uniform" to be worn by everyone on the trip at specific times. They can be plain white or colored t-shirts imprinted with a design commemorating your trip. Or maybe they could be a solid color polo style with a design imprinted or embroidered on the left front. You might want to have different colors for students, chaperones, and instructors. Usually buying a large quantity will reduce the cost quite a bit.

Action Plan For This Month:

- *Begin to assemble the items needed to pack effectively: zip-lock bags, etc.*
- *Check over lists to see if you have all the needed items*
- *Fill out and turn in any remaining forms that are needed*

MARCH MEETING: GROUP LOGISTICS, TRIP JOBS, GAME

At this meeting you will want to discuss group logistics: loading and unloading, seating arrangements on buses, and trip jobs. You may also want to discuss some shopping tips and may want to try the "money game" if you will be using foreign currency.

For the "money game" you will want to gather several different items that might be purchased as souvenirs on the trip. You might be able to find somebody that has returned from the countries you will be visiting and may have some souvenirs they would be willing to let you borrow. Be sure to ask them if they remember what they paid for them. Set these items up on a table. Write down the amount that each one was purchased for on a card, the foreign currency amount on one side and the value in American dollars on the other. Have the foreign currency amount showing towards the audience.

The purpose of the game is to help familiarize the travelers with the prices in foreign currency and what the values are in American dollars. You might want to have a poster-sized chart of foreign currency amounts and their values in American dollars. It would be helpful if you can show some of the actual foreign currency, including coins. Then ask the audience to guess what the cost of each item equals in American money.

After they guess show them what the real cost is in American money. Everyone can then see how close they came in guessing the right amount. If they are having trouble in getting the right amounts you might want to go over the poster chart of foreign currency and explain how to convert to American currency.

If you will be using more than one type of foreign currency you may want to set this up for all these different currencies. You may need different souvenirs from each country, or you may be able to use the same ones. You will need additional currency poster charts however.

If you can get currency converter charts off the Internet or from your Travel Agent, you may want to print up enough for everyone to have a copy and hand them out at this meeting. If you will be using more than one foreign currency be sure to get a chart for each one. Even with the advent of the Euro if you are going to England you may still need to get English pounds. For our England Trip we flew out of Canada so we had to deal with Canadian money too. American money was accepted but change was given in Canadian money.

Tour Buses

At this meeting you will need to discuss some of the logistics in traveling with a large group and have everyone sign up as needed. The first logistic is concerned with the tour bus assignments. If your whole group will fit on one bus then you don't have to concern yourself with this. However, if your group is large enough for two or more buses it will probably be helpful to make bus assignments now, so everyone is accounted for and will know where to go. The easiest way is to have sign-up sheets for each bus. Be sure to find out the maximum number of seats available on each bus. Have the chaperones and instructors sign up first, spreading themselves evenly among all the buses. Students sign up then. Remind them that they will need to stay on their assigned bus throughout the trip. There should be no changing buses unless chaperones on both buses agree.

It really is a lot easier to have assigned buses for everyone especially if you are doing lots of sightseeing and getting in and out of the buses a lot. You can be flexible however and allow them to change buses if they have the permission of both sets of chaperones on each bus. I have found that this is usually not a big problem and that only a few will want to change throughout the whole trip. You just want to have a way to ensure that you will not leave anyone behind at your various stops. You will need to count everyone **every** time you are leaving a stop. Having assigned buses makes this a whole lot easier on everyone.

Assigned seats are usually not needed. People are such creatures of habit that they usually go back to the same seat. This can be very helpful in counting because you can immediately see who is not there.

If your group will be on different flights, at different times, you may need to have different bus assignments for that transportation than for the tour buses. Also, there may be different sized buses for the trip to and from the airport at your destination. You will need to adjust the bus assignments for these situations as needed. Sometimes assigned buses may seem like a big hassle and may simply not be possible at certain times (you may need to load the buses very quickly to leave from the airport to your next destination). You still need to do an accurate count every time the buses are leaving somewhere. The total of the numbers on each bus should always add up to the total in that particular group. If there are separate groups because of different flights there always needs to be someone in charge of the group with good communication among the adults that are a part of that group. They all need to know who is to be in that group and the total number of people in that particular group. This will save you a lot of frustration in trying to determine if everyone is there and ready to go.

Trip Jobs

Moving a large group of travelers from place to place quickly and easily can be achieved with a certain amount of planning. To move things along it is very helpful to have assigned jobs for everyone on the trip. You can ask the students to sign up for jobs before they leave on the trip. Various jobs would include loading and unloading the luggage on the buses, taking luggage off luggage carousels at the airport, cleaning up the buses at the end of each day, loading and unloading instruments, setting up and breaking down concert sites, packing up the instruments for the flights.

Action Plan For This Month:

- *Arrange to obtain foreign currency for the countries you will be visiting*
- *Sign up for tour buses*
- *Sign up for trip jobs*

APRIL MEETING: RULES AND GUIDELINES, DEPARTURE DAY

At this meeting I would have the Leader discuss with everyone who will be going on the trip, as well as with all of the parents, the Student Rules and Guidelines for Behavior that are expected on this trip. All Rules and Guidelines need to be clearly explained and any consequences of behavior that is not appropriate need to be carefully spelled out. Copies of these should be given to both students and parents. It is very important that you have plenty of time to go over the Rules and Guidelines and make sure everyone has time to get their questions answered. Remind them that in signing the Trip Contract they agreed to abide by these Rules.

At this meeting you will also need to discuss several other things. You will also want to hand out copies of the **final itinerary** for students and parents, with pertinent phone numbers. Then you will want to give specific instructions for departure day and return day. If you are using Passports you might want everyone to hand in their Passports to you at this time if you are choosing to have the Leader carry them all the time except when they are needed. You will also want to have a time when parents can meet with their student's assigned chaperones. They would be able discuss any concerns they have about their student as well as discuss how they as a family have handled the finances, etc. for the trip so the chaperones will know how to best fulfill their role.

This is also a time when you will want to hand out all the prepared paperwork and forms that the chaperones will need to carry on the trip. It is very helpful for the chaperones to receive this ahead of time so they can arrange to pack it in their carry-on.

This meeting may need to be on a different day than the other meetings have been because of the date of the departure date of the trip. It may also need to be earlier in the month than the others have been. If you are leaving on a Thursday you may want to have the meeting on the Monday night before that. It is recommended that you not have it any later in the week if you can help it. You might even want it during the week before.

If you are having some sort of pre-trip performance you might want to schedule this a few weeks before the departure date. This will give you plenty of time to pack up the instruments and uniforms and will not make the week before the trip so hectic.

PART TWO: PREPARING FOR THE TRIP

CHAPTER 5
-
TRAVEL DOCUMENTS

OBTAINING TRAVEL DOCUMENTS

Passports

Passports are an essential element of international travel and everyone will need to have one. You will want to explain exactly what is needed to obtain a Passport: certified birth certificate, special Passport pictures, the amount of money needed, and a parent with them if the student is under 16. Passports for children under 16 usually cost less, $40 at this time but are only good for 5 years. Over age 16 they are good for 10 years and cost $55 at this time. You will have to pay a separate fee of $30 per Passport for the Execution Fee. The total fee will then be $70 for under 16 and $85 for over 16. A renewal costs $55 and can be used only on a Passport for someone who is renewing a Passport that was issued when they were over 16 and not more than 15 years ago. Parents might want to consider when they want their student to apply for the Passport. However, you need to encourage them to get the application done at least 3 months prior to the departure date of the trip. It usually takes about a month to get the Passport and the birth certificate returned.

For up to date Passport information and an application that you can download from the United State Government check the website at http://www.travel.state.gov.

Parents will need to consider too if their student is eager to get their driver's license during this time, since the birth certificate will be unavailable for the period of time they are waiting for everything to be returned with the Passport. At a few of your meetings you might want to arrange for a Passport photographer to be there an hour or so before your meeting begins to take Passport pictures, perhaps at a reduced price. Also, have a sheet prepared listing the places they may apply for a Passport, usually Post Offices, but occasionally Police Stations, the times and days they are open, and maybe addresses and phone numbers.

Sometimes you may be able to get an "expressed" Passport in a very short period of time, but this will usually cost quite a bit more, $60 at this time.

You will want to tell everyone that they will need to make 5 copies of the information pages of the Passport, and then turn 2 of them in at the December meeting. These copies will be used as follows: 1 will be carried by the Leader of the group, or his designee, even if the Leader collects and carries the Passports during the trip; 1 will be carried by the assigned chaperone, 1 will be carried by the student or adult; another 1 needs to be in the luggage, and 1 needs to stay home with the rest of the family.

Having this many copies will be very helpful if a Passport is lost or stolen. A lot of groups have the Leader carry the students' Passports and the other adults too, if they wish, when they aren't needed for entering or leaving a country. The Passports need to be in a locked case, possibly with the airline tickets, and stored in a secure place (hotel safe), or carried with the Leader at **all times.**

Ziplock bags labeled with the chaperone's name and a list of the students assigned to him or her can hold the Passports and make it easier to hand them back in to the Leader, and easy to hand out as needed.

Each person needs to have at least a copy of their Passport identification page with them at all times, for identification. In addition, it is always a good idea to have another copy in your luggage.

As an added safeguard it is a good idea to have the chaperones carry copies of the Passports of the students they are assigned to. Chaperones can either have the "head chaperone" carry a copy of theirs, or another friend on the trip carry it.

Picture Identification Card

It is also necessary for each person to carry a Picture Identification Card with him or her, in addition to the Passport. This is especially true if they will not be carrying their Passports with them at all times. The Picture Identification is needed for boarding the plane, and sometimes for purchasing items, and for cashing Travelers Checks.

The Picture Identification Card is usually a Driver's License. If a student is too young to have a Driver's License they can get a Picture Identification Card at the Department of Motor Vehicles for a small fee. You will want to check with the DMV but you usually need to bring a certified birth certificate with you and the parent may need to accompany their child.

Students may think that their Student Body Card with their picture on it would suffice for this, but I have found that especially in foreign countries this type of card was not accepted. Airports are getting much stricter on identification.

Students will need to make 4 copies of their I.D. Card, since they will be carrying the card with them at all times, in their money belt, or wallet when necessary. They should also have a copy in their luggage. One copy will be with the Leader, one copy with their assigned chaperone and one copy will be left at home.

Frequent Flyer Miles

The Travel Agent should be able to explain to your group how to receive Frequent Flyer Miles for your trip. He/she should tell you which airlines you will be traveling on, and which, if any, other airlines may have a reciprocal agreement so they will honor each others Frequent Flyer Miles. You will need to contact the airline yourself and sign up for the Frequent Flyer Program. They will send you a member number that you will need to give to the Travel Agent to receive your miles.

If your group happens to have to travel on different airlines for your trip you will need to decide who will be on each airline as soon as possible so they will have time to sign up for a Frequent Flyer Program.

Special Power of Attorney

While the Special Power of Attorney may not seem to be a "Travel Document" as such, I would suggest that no matter what type of trip you are going on if you are taking students you need some type of "Special Power of Attorney" for each student. This form gives the person or persons listed (usually the Leader and/or chaperones) permission from the parents of the student listed to take their student on the trip. It also directs them to act on behalf of the parents in the best interests of the student.

Since most of the students going on the trip will probably be considered minors they need someone to be able to act in the capacity of their parents if they are in a situation where they need this. Hopefully these situations would not occur: being arrested for possession of illegal drugs or underage drinking, fighting, committing a crime or being a victim of a crime, or even having their money or Passport stolen.

This form needs to be **notarized** so parents need to be given this form quite a bit ahead of time so they have plenty of time to get it notarized. If by chance someone in your group, or maybe parents or others is a Notary you might ask them to come to one of your meetings and be available to notarize these forms. Be sure to allow plenty of time for this!!!

The Leader will need to be one of the designated adults as well as possibly the assigned chaperone for each student.

CHAPTER 6

-

LUGGAGE AND TRAVEL ITEMS

LUGGAGE

The first thing that you need to consider about luggage would be to decide what is the largest suitcase you can carry while fully packed. It may need to be smaller than you think. Wheels are wonderful, and save you a lot of energy, but you may end up in a housing situation where you do not have elevators and you have to carry all your luggage up several flights of stairs. This happened to our group in England when we stayed at the University of Bristol. It was a great place to stay, but had no elevators with several flights of stairs to navigate. If you have trouble carrying your suitcase very far it is probably too big and too heavy for you to manage on a long trip. Don't forget that you'll be carrying your carry-on and daypack along with the suitcase, probably all at the same time.

Suitcases get really banged around being dragged up and down stairs and shoved in and pulled out of luggage bins in buses, so make sure the luggage you get will be able to withstand this treatment.

Your suitcase does need to be large enough for you to be able to carry all your clothes, shoes, and other necessities, as well as have lots of room for souvenirs. It is amazing how much room souvenirs can take up! When I was in England my roommate had to leave behind her big fluffy towel to make room for her souvenirs. We had to take our own towels to use when we stayed in the hostels, but our last two nights were in a hotel where they provided towels. My friend preferred her new souvenirs to her old towel. A towel can be replaced but souvenirs from around the world cannot! Just remember to consider how much the suitcase will weigh when fully loaded too.

Look for sturdy wheels, heavy-duty fabric, and strong zippers, along with a very sturdy extendable handle to pull the suitcase with. Sometimes suitcases can be expanded by unzipping a section around the edges of the suitcase. This can be a very handy feature on your way back. Carry-ons may have wheels too, and need to have plenty of space and handy pockets. Make sure your carry-on is well under the dimensions required by the airlines...usually 14" X 22" X 8". Sometimes carry-ons are exactly these dimensions to begin with, but if you put anything in the outside pockets it ends up being too big.

When I bought my large traveling suitcase it came with a carry-on that was these exact dimensions. I thought about this a lot, and eventually bought another similar carry-on that was about 2" smaller. Luckily for me it was on a special sale so I got a good deal, since I had waited, and worried, until about a week before the trip. I was so glad I did because I stuffed that carry-on so full on the way home it was almost to the required dimensions, but I really needed that space for souvenirs. The other one would not have worked for me.

I suggest that you also have some sort of daypack for everyday sightseeing, and to have access to on the airplane. This can be a small backpack, a fanny pack, or a tote bag. Something that you can put the things in you need just for that day: camera and extra film, snacks, water, sunglasses, small first aid kit, notepad, pen, tissues, sunscreen, itinerary. A bag to hold just your camera and film is really helpful too. A fanny pack can work great for this. You can wear it, so the camera is always handy, and carry your daypack too, if you want. Then just put the fanny pack into the daypack when you need to.

You will need to get suggestions from your Travel Agent as to any weight or amount restrictions on the luggage. Usually you are allowed two checked suitcases, one carry-on bag, and one other item: purse, briefcase, per person. If your group is bringing along a lot of extra items: musical instruments and uniform cases, you may be limited to one checked suitcase per person, and only one carry-on. There may be additional weight restrictions too. Find out all these details and make sure everyone in your group understands the limitations. You might consider bringing an accurate scale to your meetings and let everyone weigh their fully packed suitcases and carry-ons if you have concerns about weight.

TRAVEL ITEMS:

There are many unique items that are tremendously useful while traveling. They may seem to be just an extra expense but I have found the following to be especially useful. I have used a money belt on trips in the U.S. too.

Travel Guidebook

One of the first things I would suggest you get after you decide you are going on a trip is a travel guidebook for the country or countries that you will be visiting. A travel guidebook will not only give you information about the country and the sights you will be seeing but will provide you with lots of useful tips about the customs and particulars. Specifically you should find information on the type of electricity used, time zones, how to use the public telephones and restrooms, currency used and availability of ATM's.

A recent travel guidebook should have information about cellular phone coverage and Internet availability. There may be cyber cafes near where you will be staying or visiting where you can check your email. Hotels where you might be staying may also have Internet access.

Foreign Language Translation Book

If you are going to a foreign country where you do not know the language you will want to take a foreign language translation book. Be sure to become familiar with the book before you leave on the trip.

There are also electronic Foreign Language Translators. These are about the size of a small calculator, and could be very handy. Learn how to use it before you leave, so you will be able to use it with ease when you get there.

Electricity Converter

Most foreign countries that you will be visiting may have different electrical plugs than we have in the United States. In some countries even the actual electrical voltage is different than what our appliances use (110 in the U.S. as opposed to 240 in Europe). It is important that you find out from your Travel Agent what the countries you will be visiting require for electricity and plugs.

For example, on my trip to Mexico the plugs there were of the two-prong type, but without the polarized side (wider blade on the plug). Many of our appliances: hair dryers, razors, curling irons could not be plugged in. In England they have a different type of voltage than the United States so we needed a converter. Their plugs are different too, so we needed an adapter too. Continental Europe uses an entirely different type of plug.

You can buy a special converter kit that has a converter and several different types of adapter plugs where travel items are sold. Usually there will be a display next to the area where luggage is sold. Most department stores will have a display of travel items, as well as some office supply stores. Luggage specialty shops will also have them. These items rarely go on sale, but sometimes they do so you will need to watch for sales.

With the converter and/or the adapter plugs you should be able to use most of your appliances. Unfortunately sometimes the appliance cannot handle the change. In England a hair dryer started smoking, and set off the smoke detectors and the alarms in the hostel where we were staying. My friend's curling iron also shorted out, even with the converter and adapter. She didn't want to be without one so she bought one there, and now has a nice souvenir that won't work here!

Check your appliances before you leave...some will actually have a built-in converter, but they will still need an adapter plug. Consider if you will really need to take certain appliances. Some rechargeable razors may last for the duration of the trip. Check how long yours will last on one charge before you leave on the trip.

Most students, and adults, will not want to be without their hair dryers or curling irons, so they are going to need to purchase a converter kit with adapters. Roommates can discuss this and maybe share one, but this can get a little tricky when everyone wants to use it at the same time. There may be only a few plugs in the room where you are staying too, so roommates will need to negotiate who uses them and when. Converter kits are one of the more expensive travel items, ranging usually from $20 to $25. If you use an adapter on your appliance you might want to tape it to the plug so you don't accidentally leave it in the socket when you unplug your appliance.

Money Belt

A money belt is one of the most important items you can have to help relieve a lot of the stress concerning carrying your money and identification. It may seem like such a simple thing, and unfortunately not something that most travelers think about. However, if a wallet containing all your money, credit cards and identification is lost or stolen, you will experience an incredible amount of frustration, and those around you will too. On a trip with students this is magnified with the chaperones having to help a distraught student, or adult, replace the desperately needed items. Money may be very difficult to replace. It can happen to anyone!!!

Money belts can be purchased where luggage is sold. There are many different styles, some with a waist strap, some have a neck strap, or with a fastener that attaches to a woman's bra. They are worn under your outer clothes, but on top of your underwear. If you know it will be warm you may want to put all of your items in a ziplock bag, then inside the money belt. Otherwise you may end up with some very wet money and information cards. This happened to me in Mexico and Florida.

Items to go in the money belt include:

- all your money, except for what you will need that day (sort currency by country, put in separate snack size ziplock bags)
- ATM card
- credit card
- Passport or copy of Passport information page
- Picture Identification Card (unless you know you will need it that day)
- medical insurance card
- a card with all your important phone numbers (family and work numbers), including the numbers to call if your credit card/ATM card is lost or stolen and the account numbers

- a card with your PIN number if you're afraid you'll forget it, along with the combination to any locks you have
- you should also have a card with pertinent medical information on it too; include any diagnosis, medications you are taking, and, especially, list any allergies

A few index cards will work well for all the phone numbers, other information and the medical history.

You will need some kind of small wallet or change purse to carry the money you need for the day. Even if this is stolen or lost, it is not as bad as having all of your valuables and identification gone.

Luggage Tags

Every bag you take with you should have some type of luggage tag on it with your name, address and phone number. This is vital to help your luggage to be returned to you if it accidentally goes somewhere else and is not there when you try to retrieve it from baggage check. It's also important to have a tag on your carry-on bag. These bags can get separated from you in loading them on your tour bus, or just waiting for your next transportation. I can't remember how many times I've seen a student just put down a bag and then walk off and leave it while busy talking or eating. A chaperone had to pick it up and search inside for some form of identification to get it back to the right person.

There should also be some form of a luggage tag on the daypack too. If you have a separate camera bag it would be wise to have a tag on that too. The tag should have the owner's name, address and phone number on it. Some people worry about putting their home address and phone number on a luggage tag in case a thief gets it and then knows the owner is not home and may try to burglarize their home. This is very unlikely, especially since in all probability it will not be stolen. However, if this is a concern have a business address on the tag, but do have the correct travelers' name. The luggage tags really help to make it easier for the group of travelers to check bags to see if they belong with the group and to get them to the right person.

I would also encourage everyone to have a 3x5 card with his or her name, address and phone number printed on it taped inside **every** bag. Sometimes luggage tags get ripped off the bags in handling, or simply become unattached. Then if an airline opens the bag they will be able to know to whom the bag belongs and can return it.

Another thing to do that is extremely helpful is to have some identifying mark on all your pieces of luggage. This can be a sticker, a thick piece of yarn, fabric, or ribbon tied to the handle, a flashy key chain hung on the zipper pull, a brightly colored luggage tag. So many pieces of luggage look just alike so it is very helpful to have a quick way to tell which one is yours.

To illustrate this have several people bring their luggage to one of your meetings. You'll be surprised how many will have black rolling suitcases that all look alike.

When I went to Mexico with a group of students and two of my sons, our luggage was just alike. We had different colored thick pieces of yarn tied around the handles so we could tell which one was ours. My boys certainly didn't want to get their mom's luggage!

Students may not be familiar with their luggage either, so if they put something personal on it they will be more likely to recognize it later.

I would also suggest that you provide to the whole group pieces of brightly colored yarn to tie onto the handles of their luggage. This will be very helpful when pulling the checked baggage off the luggage carousel. You can easily tell which pieces of luggage belong with your group. If you think it will be helpful you might color code the yarn according to the buses to keep the luggage with the assigned bus.

Luggage Locks

Usually luggage will come with tiny locks and keys. You will need to decide if these locks will be sturdy enough. A lot of times they are pretty flimsy. The purpose of luggage locks is simply to slow down any would-be thief. If thieves really want to get into your luggage, they will. The locks may deter the thief from taking the time to deal with them however.

Therefore you will want some sort of locks, either key or combination, on your checked and carry-on bags. Not only will you want to lock your luggage while traveling on the plane, train or bus, but also you may want to lock the bags you leave in your hotel room when you are out sightseeing. You want to be careful without being paranoid.

I would suggest that you take both keys with you, kept in two different places, just in case one gets lost. It's no fun to have to find someone to pry open the lock if you lose the key. I usually carry one on a small key chain in the outside pocket of the bag it goes to. You may have other things in the pocket, dirty laundry is nice, so if anyone were looking for the key it wouldn't be immediately evident. Having this one with the bag is really helpful if you are asked to open it to be searched at a security checkpoint. Then you don't have to go searching in your other bags for the key. This actually happened to me in Mexico and I was so thankful that I didn't have to search very far for the key. With the additional security now in airports it is quite possible that you will have to open your bags to be searched, so the handier the better. The other key could be kept in a purse, money belt or daypack, on a key chain. These keys are so tiny you really need some sort of key chain to keep track of them.

Combination locks are great so that you don't have to keep track of keys. However, you do need to write down that combination and keep it in your money belt. You need to have it written down somewhere in case you get rattled when you are asked to open your bags for a search and can't remember anything. If you have two or more different combination locks be sure you write them all down and indicate which combination belongs to which lock.

THEFT

Unfortunately, pickpockets and thieves are everywhere, and American tourists are a favorite prey. You just need to remind everyone to be careful and thoughtful in his or her behavior. In traveling with a group you will be a very conspicuous target so you will need to be especially careful. A group cannot simply melt into the community the way one or two tourists can.

Students are notoriously known for being easily distracted when they are talking or eating. They need to remember to be aware of their surroundings and their belongings, and where they are at all times. A friend's daughter was standing up talking to her friends in an airport. She had just taken some pictures and had placed her camera on top of her backpack. She looked down a few minutes later and it was gone. Thieves are very quick.

As stated before, carry only the cash needed for that day's expenses in your wallet. If you know you will be using a credit card or an ATM card that day, put it in. Otherwise keep all your other money and cards in your money belt.

Try to carry the wallet as close to your body as possible. An inside pocket is best. Men should not carry a wallet in a back pocket. Not only is this hard on your back when you are sitting for long periods of time but this is the easiest place for a pickpocket to get at it. It may be awkward at first, but your front pants pocket is best.

Women, if you want to carry a purse with your wallet inside get one with a long strap and have the strap go across your body, not over your shoulder. A thief can easily run by you and grab your purse off your shoulder. If your purse is small you can wear it all the time this way, even when you are eating, and you will know right where it is and no one can snatch it.

If you are carrying a daypack make sure you have nothing valuable in the small outside pocket. Someone can open this and reach inside while you are busy sightseeing. The other items will probably be far enough down inside the bag to be OK but I wouldn't carry my wallet there. I would also not carry anything really valuable in there either. Always consider if you will be willing to lose the items you are carrying in the daypack. If you aren't, don't bring them.

Some people like to wear fanny packs. These are very handy for carrying things, especially cameras, because they are easy to get into, and your hands are free. However, be careful of carrying your money in the outside zippered pockets. A thief can distract you and easily grab your wallet, especially if you have left if unzipped while you are using your camera, or even bargaining with someone selling things. This happened to a student on a trip while she was trying to bargain with someone. They stood very close and nudged up against her. She had left the zipper open because she had just checked to see how much money she had. She had taken some of her money out and was holding it in her hand as she was bargaining. She wasn't paying any attention to the fanny pack, and the thief reached in and took some of her money. Luckily he didn't get it all.

Your luggage locks should deter anybody handling your checked baggage at the airport, train, bus, provided that you remember to use them and the thief is in a hurry. Unfortunately, if a thief has a little time they can just cut your bag open. Hopefully this will not happen to you.

CLOTHES

Your Travel Agent should be able to tell you approximate temperatures and weather conditions for the countries and places you will be visiting. This will help you in planning the wardrobe you will want to take on the trip. There are several considerations that you will want to take into account.

First you will want to consider the weather where you will be leaving, and where you will be arriving. Sometimes the temperatures can be quite different, so you will want to consider this when planning your traveling attire. Layering your clothes can be the answer to a lot of temperature concerns. It may be very warm outside, but inside the plane or tour bus, the air conditioning can be very cool.

Comfort should be a main concern too. Anything tight or constricting is just not worth it. Teens love jeans but they need to consider how their jeans fit when they sit down for a long period of time. Airlines usually discourage passengers from wearing a lot of polyester and even panty hose on flights in case, heaven forbid, you need to use the emergency exit chutes (you can get a nasty burn from the friction). Chances are nothing will happen, but think about it!

If you are going to a warm climate your clothes will probably be fairly lightweight, so they will take up less space. However, you will usually need a fresh change of clothes every day. In a cool climate your clothes will be heavier and take up more space, but you may be able to mix and match certain items and possibly wear pants and jackets two or three times. You will usually want a fresh shirt or top every day, and of course, fresh changes of underwear and socks for each day you will be gone and one spare set to have in your carry-on, along with an extra outfit (pants and shirt).

My preferences on a cool climate trip are mid-weight knits with a heavier sweater for warmth if needed. If it will be especially cold (below freezing) you will want to consider wool or wool blends. A mid to heavy weight jacket, depending upon the weather, will be necessary. Consider if you will need a hat and gloves too. Water resistance is very helpful if it will be raining where you will be going. A jacket with a hood can be very helpful. A warm to hot climate needs cottons and/or cotton blends. Stay away from polyester if possible. A lightweight jacket for cool evenings and bus rides is essential. Do think about the fabrics and if they will wrinkle easily. You may not have access to an iron.

You may need certain special clothes for swimming, or going to a nice dinner, or the theatre. Shorts and long pants for women may not be acceptable attire at churches or cathedrals. Ask your Travel Agent about this. A long skirt or dress and/or a scarf or jewelry to "dress it up" for women may work just fine. Men might want to take a shirt and tie. Don't forget shoes and accessories that you will need, as well as nightclothes, and a robe and slippers if you desire. Two pairs of shoes, well broken in for walking, are very nice to have if you have enough room, though one pair will do unless you get really wet. You might want to take a fancier pair for the special night out or a performance. Don't forget sandals if you are going to the beach.

It is really important to have comfortable walking shoes that you have worn for awhile before you leave on the trip. Be sure to wear the shoes for several hours at a time while walking and being on you're feet, not just sitting around. Feet tend to swell when you are walking a lot, and also while you are flying on an airplane. Shoes can feel a lot different after a day's worth of sightseeing and your feet may pay the price. Aching feet, with sore spots, and blisters, can really make you feel miserable.

Your leader may have specific suggestions about the type of traveling clothes that he or she wants you to wear on the plane. He/she may want you to dress up a little, with nicer pants than jeans, and possibly a shirt with a collar, instead of just a tee shirt. Jeans can be rather binding on a long plane flight anyway, but teens love them. Or your leader may want everyone to wear the same shirt, maybe a specially designed tee shirt or polo shirt, with nice pants on the plane going and possibly coming back. Some may even prefer that everyone wear long pants on the plane, even when leaving a warm climate. These things need to be discussed with the group beforehand and expectations need to be made very clear.

If there are any concerns about the style of clothes that will be worn this will need to be discussed too. There may be concerns that the students will dress too casually (tee shirts and jeans) for certain situations (museums, cathedrals etc), or possibly too scantily in hot climates. These concerns need to be addressed and the guidelines made very clear. I have heard of situations when there were arguments over how wide the girls straps were on the tops they were wearing. Also, discuss if one piece or two piece swimsuits are allowed.

Other areas of concern might by shirts with inappropriate sayings on them, ragged or holes in clothing (sometimes that's the style!) or simply sloppy looking outfits. Some things are not worth getting into big arguments over, but sometimes there may be situations where lines must be drawn because teens will try to push the limits or they just may not have a clue that they look inappropriate. There are usually more concerns when you are going to hot climates, so be aware. Sometimes young men may need to be reminded not to wear the same shirt everyday.

Here are some suggestions for the amount of clothes to take if your trip is longer than 7 or 8 days and you plan on washing some or all of the clothes you are taking. If your trip is between 6 and 8 days you may be able to take enough extra clothes to not have to do any washing and still not have too much in your suitcase. Otherwise you may want to try to mix and match your clothing and take the least amount that you can possibly get by with or absolutely need.

Minimum Amount of Clothes to Mix and Match:

- 5 shirts
- 2-3 pants
- 1-2 overshirts or jackets
- 1 sweater
- extra pair of shoes
- 5 sets of underwear and socks
- nightclothes
- 1 light to mid-weight jacket with a hood

Optional:
- shorts
- tie or scarf
- swimsuit
- sandals

Women:
- long or short skirt
- 2 or 3 bras

If you plan on washing clothes you will also need to take a clothesline, laundry soap (liquid dissolves better, but wrap the bottle in a ziplock bag) and a few plastic hangars. Some housing sites may have laundry and dry-cleaning services but you will have to pay for them. You may be able to find a Laundromat but it may be difficult for everyone to get his or her laundry done in a short amount of time. Remind parents to give their students instructions on washing clothes in a sink and hanging them up to dry. Be sure to take a few large ziplock or plastic bags to put wet or damp laundry in if it doesn't dry overnight.

You will also need to consider how easily the clothes you are taking will be to wash and dry on your trip. Heavy cottons may not dry quickly enough. There are wonderful fabrics available now that are comfortable, and dry very quickly, but you may not have outfits in these fabrics. There are companies that make clothes especially for traveling: Exofficio and Tilley are popular brands. They are wonderful clothes but can be a bit pricey. Don't forget to think about the underwear and socks that you will be taking and if they will wash and dry easily enough too.

Remember you are not only representing your school or organization, but also your hometown, your state and the United States of America while you are traveling in foreign countries. People will be looking at you!

Performance Clothes

If your group will be doing performances you will need to consider the special clothes that you will need, and if these will need to be packed in your own luggage, or be shipped in special uniform/shipping boxes. These special clothes may take up quite a bit of room so you need to plan for this. Also you will need to consider how many times you will need to wear these performance clothes, and if you will need to bring an extra set. For example, if yours is a concert band and the students wear black pants or skirts and white shirts or tops you may need to bring extras if you will be performing more than two or three times and/or need to wear them for very long periods of time before or after the performances. Don't forget nicer shoes and socks if you need them.

If students will be changing on the bus or at the performance I encourage you to have them pack their performance clothes in a lightweight garment bag, with their name on it, so they may carry it with them. Remind them to take hangars. This will help them to keep all the clothes for the performance together and will protect the clothes while traveling. They can also put their street clothes in the bag while they are not wearing them.

If the performance clothes are being shipped in special containers or boxes, garment bags are still very helpful in keeping each performer's clothes separate, with their individual items all together. Don't forget to have names on garment bags! Wide masking tape with the name written on it works well.

Costumes/Props

If you are taking costumes and/or props, possibly for a theatrical performance, you will need to consider how best to transport them. For more elaborate costumes and props you may need to make arrangements for a more secure shipment for these items. Be sure all costumes are marked with the performer's name even in separate garment bags. Smaller or simpler costumes may be carried in the individual's luggage, and should also be marked with the performer's name in case of separation from personal belongings.

Uniforms

If you are taking special uniforms you will need to decide how the uniforms need to be packed. If they are large uniforms, such as band uniforms, you may want to have special packing containers just for them. If they are smaller you may want each person to pack their own.

If you are a sports team you may need several different sets of uniforms for each person. You may want to pack these all together too, and then arrange for laundering them and returning them to each participant as needed, or have each person responsible for their own. Practice uniforms may be needed too, as well as warm-ups to wear over the uniforms. Don't forget any special shoes and socks that might be needed.

Packing

You will want to think about how much room you will have in the suitcase and carry-on that you are planning to take with you. Don't forget to leave plenty of room for souvenirs that you will buy on your trip. Also, consider the weight of the bags once they are full of clothes, shoes, toiletries, and souvenirs. Each person going on the trip needs to remember that they will need to be able to manage all of their own luggage. Really heavy luggage can make a trip miserable, especially if you are going from place to place and the luggage is loaded and unloaded every day or so. You might have to carry them up stairs.

Several months before the trip I suggest you do a "Trial Pack" where you pick out all the clothes you think you will be taking, including any performance clothes or uniforms if you have to pack them. Don't forget shoes, socks, underwear and nightclothes! Accessories and toiletry and cosmetic bags need to go in too, as well as a laundry bag and possibly a towel. Think about what appliances you may need to take: hair dryer, curling iron, razor. They also take up space.

Try putting everything in the suitcase, carry-on and daypack that you plan on taking. This will give you a good idea if the luggage you have chosen to take are really going to hold everything, with some room to spare, or if you need to get something else. This will also give you an idea if the clothes you think you want to take really are going to meet your needs on the trip. You may find out that those outfits really aren't going to work, or that you don't have as many as you thought. You will find out if you have enough sets of underwear and socks too. You may not.

Almost everyone I know who went on the major trips I went on bought at least some new underwear and socks, night clothes, and usually a few new outfits. It will be helpful to have a preliminary itinerary in front of you as you pick out your outfits. That way you won't forget the special dinners, theatre, etc. that may require particular clothes.

Please don't wait to do this until the week before the trip. You may be in for an expensive surprise and/or a lot of unhappiness if you need to have a lot of new items of clothing, and/or a new suitcase right before the trip. There may not be enough money available to get all that you want.

Consider too the length of the trip. If the trip is around a week or less you can usually get by with one suitcase and your carry-on. If the trip is longer you may need another suitcase for additional clothes, or you may have to do some laundry. This is not the easiest thing with a group of students, so you will have to do some additional planning in the itinerary for your trip to allow for time and places to do laundry.

Don't forget to check out your toiletry and cosmetic cases too. You may need more room than you think. Start looking for travel sized items now so you won't have to buy them all later. If there are some items you know that there aren't travel sizes available (cosmetics) consider the items you are now using and when they are down to about 1/3 to 1/4 left in them set them aside for travel. You will save some on weight this way, and then will always have your travel things ready to go. You can also buy plastic containers to hold your toothbrush, soap, as well as small plastic bottles to decant some of your toiletry items into.

CHAPTER 7

-

FINANCES

TRIP BUDGET AND FINANCES

Families have many different ideas about money and how to budget on a trip. Each family needs to discuss this area with their student and make sure everyone understands each other's expectations. Sometimes on a trip like this it will be really hard to know how much one will want to spend on souvenirs until they are actually there and see what all is available. For students who have not been away on a trip without their parents before, and have not really had to handle much money by themselves, this can be quite challenging. Having to budget for several extra meals individually can only add to all this. Snacks and beverages also need to be planned for.

I would hope that your Travel Agent would be somewhat familiar with the sights you will be seeing and the souvenir opportunities that will be available. Most of the major attractions that you will be visiting will have souvenir shops. A good number of your travelers will want to buy at least something at each of these stops. Your agent will be able to give you an idea of some of the items available for purchase and a rough estimate of what they will cost.

If you are on a very tight budget you might want to buy small items such as key chains, magnets, pens, from each place. Postcards are wonderful too, especially since you may not be able to take pictures inside some places. Most spots will have books about the attraction that make wonderful souvenirs to look at later, but they can be a bit expensive. Some people like to build collections of items commemorating the places they are visiting: spoons, letter openers, thimbles, mugs. Others will be looking for specific things that they have heard about and want to bring back: lace, wool items, teapots, tea, clocks, Christmas ornaments.

It will be helpful if you look at the itinerary and consider each of the places you will be visiting. From what the Travel Agent has said, and possibly other speakers too, try to estimate what you might want to spend. Some places, for example, the Tower of London (a very special sight seeing spot) you will decide are major places where you will probably want to spend more on souvenirs. You might want to buy a couple of books and several small items (letter opener, miniature suit of arms, for you and for gifts). Other places you may only want to pick up a few postcards and possibly a key chain.

A budget plan is really helpful to help you remember what sights may be coming up on your journey. You may have some really special attractions towards the end of your trip that you will want to make sure you have enough money left to buy souvenirs at.

On my trip to Mexico one of the last sights we visited was a quaint town called Taxco where there were lots of sterling silver items available at incredible prices. Unfortunately some of the students had spent most of their money so were unable to buy many items.

Don't forget gifts for others too. It is really fun to buy things for friends and family back at home, and they are really excited when you get home and have gifts for them. Do remember to buy things for yourself too. I've seen people get so caught up in getting gifts for others that they forget to get things for themselves. They get home and then are disappointed that they don't have any souvenirs left for themselves.

Remember that each person may only bring back (items shipped home count too) items valued up to $400 total that will be tax-free. Anything over that amount will be taxed at the 10% rate and this tax will need to be paid at Customs after you reenter the United States. Keep this in mind as you are planning your budget.

Have your Travel Agent find out if there are things that you are not allowed to bring out of the countries you are visiting, or items that you are not allowed to bring into the United States (alcohol products, plants, seeds). Be sure all your travelers understand this before they leave on the trip.

Do have a little extra earmarked for emergencies too. You may spill something on yourself and have to buy a new top. Or you may need to buy more film, or batteries, or even shampoo, as well as an extra meal or two. Sometimes a provided meal just doesn't work out and you have to buy one you hadn't planned on. You may need to buy more snacks and bottled water than you had thought about.

Try to be generous with your spending money budget. This is a trip of a lifetime and you want to be able to buy some of the things you see and want to bring home. Encourage the parents of the students to make sure their children have a reasonable amount of spending money for souvenirs as well as enough for meals and snacks and beverages.

If you are on your own for some of the meals you will need to budget very carefully for these. You don't want to run out of money when you have a few meals left to pay for on your trip. You will have to be especially careful with the students in this area because they may be tempted to buy a lot of souvenirs and then go without meals. Don't forget snacks and bottled water too. Some may want to bring some snacks from home (granola bars) but they will still need to buy some snacks and beverages. Everyone may get hungrier than they will expect because of all the walking that they are doing and they all need to be especially careful to keep themselves well hydrated.

I always tried to keep my budgeted money for meals and souvenirs separate, so I would know how I was doing. I would keep meal money in one pocket of my money belt, and souvenir money in another. In my wallet I would only carry the days' budgeted money, in separate areas for meals and souvenirs. I did carry, and use, a credit card for major purchases. But I did try to stay within my budgeted amounts generally. When I was low on cash I used an ATM machine, but I had planned on having a little extra in that account just in case.

Suggested meal amounts, including tax and tip (discuss tipping amounts with your agent): Breakfast - $5-$8; Lunch - $10; Dinner - $15-$20; Snacks and beverages - $5-$10 per day. These amounts may vary a lot from place to place, so it is helpful to get advice from those who have been there before you go. People do eat varying amounts too, but these are pretty average estimates of what you will spend on meals.

Suggested Budget

FRIDAY					
Meals	Budget	Actual	*Souvenirs*	Budget	Actual
Dinner	$15	$13	Warwick Castle (major sight)	$30	$32 (Book gifts)
Snacks	$5	$4			
			Soccer Game (performance)	$10	$8 (Scarf)
SATURDAY					
Meals	Budget	Actual	*Souvenirs*	Budget	Actual
Lunch	$10	$8	Chester Tour	$5	$4(magnet)
Snacks	$5	$6	Iron Bridge	$25	$23(Book, Gifts)
SUNDAY					
Meals	Budget	Actual	*Souvenirs*	Budget	Actual
Lunch	$10	$7	Stonehenge (major sight)	$40	$50 (Books, cards, gifts)
Dinner	$15	$12			
Snacks	$5	$5			
Total	**$65**	**$55**		**$110**	**$117**

For these three days this person has spent $10 less than budgeted for meals and snacks, and has spent $7 more than budgeted for souvenirs. So they have $3 extra in their budget to spend during the rest of the trip.

You may want to make up a chart like this of estimated expenses, and then have each family fill in what they would like to spend. Travelers can then carry it with them and at the end of each day figure out how they are doing. Just remember that they are estimated expenses and in the reality of the trip expenses might be somewhat different. It just helps to think through the possible trip expenses and plan for them.

ATM's can usually be found all over the place, except right when you need them, of course. So you need to plan ahead how you will handle your finances, and have a few backup plans. I recommend that you take with you at least a few days amount of money in the currency of the countries you will be visiting. With the advent of the Euro in so many countries in Europe this makes this much easier. England still uses the Pound however, so if you will be traveling there, as well as other European countries you will want to take some Pounds with you as well as some Euros. Bear in mind that you will be charged a certain amount to change your money before you leave, and you will also have ATM charges too if you use them, which can really add up. Check with your bank to find out what these charges might be. This may help you determine how much foreign money you will want to take with you in order to avoid many extra charges.

Remember to plan on how much American money you need to take too. You may have to buy meals and/or snacks in the airport before you take off, or you might need it for other things. Some countries even prefer American money. Just be careful of the Exchange Rate.

ATM Cards

I usually like to change most of my budgeted money before I leave home. That way I don't have to worry about finding an ATM until later on in the trip when I might need more cash. ATM's do abound but sometimes it is hard to find them when you are traveling from place to place with a large group and sometimes it is impossible to leave the group to look. Also, your own group may create long lines trying to change money, causing many of you to miss seeing the very sights you came to see.

Traveling with a large group of students limits you in some of the flexibility you would have with a small group. You can't have people taking off on their own when you are in a large group activity.

.*Warning*: be sure to check with your bank to make sure your ATM card will work in a foreign country. This is especially true for students. The pins need to be numerical, and the cards usually need to be tied to a checking account. Sometimes students have ATM cards that are tied to a savings account only and they may not work overseas. Also, be sure to check the expiration date on the card and make sure it will not expire when you will be gone.

Be sure to write down on an index card the account number and the number to call if the card is lost or stolen and carry this in your money belt. The number is on the back of the card, but it won't help you much if it is gone and you don't know what number to call or the account number.

When I was in England with 103 students several of them had ATM cards that would not work over there. One was a very good friend of my son's so we loaned him money, but it was very upsetting to him. His dad was very unhappy when he found out the card didn't work because he had repeatedly asked the bank employees if it would work in England, and they had assured him that it would. When he finally was able to talk to a manager after his son had called and said it wouldn't work, the manager said that his particular kind wouldn't work and he wished that they had been able to talk to him about it. So make sure you talk to someone knowledgeable.

This situation was also compounded by the difference in time zones. Every time the son could call home he had to leave messages because his parents were at work. Then his dad had to try to call ahead to a place where we were to be staying at in order to leave a message for his son. It took several days until he could actually talk to his dad on the phone.

Credit Cards

Credit cards usually work great but it is helpful to have your picture identification with you and the name on the card needs to be the same. This is very important! Women traveling without their husbands need to have their own name on their credit card too. You will get charged the exchange rate that is on the date of your purchase. You will need to call your credit card company a few months ahead to have your student's name imprinted on a card so he/she won't have any trouble using it. Usually the credit card company will just add the student's name onto the account over the phone but sometimes they will want you to fill out an authorization form and send it to them.

Be sure to check the expiration date for the cards you will be taking to make sure they will not expire when you are away on the trip. You will have a lot of problems if they expire while you are on the trip, or if you haven't activated your new ones.

A back up credit card is also a good idea, especially if more than one of you is using one. On our England trip a mom and her twin sons were carrying a credit card from one account though each had their own name imprinted on their own card. One of the boys couldn't find his so she had to call and cancel the card. He found his card a few days later, in a shoe in his suitcase, but then they were without a valid credit card.

As you did for an ATM card, write down the credit card numbers, and the phone numbers to call if they are lost or stolen, for each card that you are carrying, on an index card to keep in your money belt. The numbers are on the back of the cards. If you don't write them down you won't know who to call or what the account numbers are.

If you will be traveling to a foreign country you may want to call your credit card company and inform them where you will be and which account number you will be using. There might be problems if you haven't used the account much and/or not in a foreign country. Usually you will not encounter any problems but you would not want to have any so it is better to call first.

Traveler's Checks

Traveler's checks are often a big headache. Sometime it is difficult to find stores that will take them, and then they charge quite a bit to cash them. You absolutely have to have a picture identification to cash them. You will need to keep the numbers in your money belt and be sure to check off those you have cashed.

Emergencies

Before your group leaves on the trip you will need to have your Committee discuss how the group will handle situations if students, and adults, have their money stolen, their ATM card doesn't work, or they run out of money because they either didn't have enough to begin with, or they got carried away in spending it, or they encounter an unfortunate emergency. These situations have happened on some of the trips I have been on, and it put the adults in very uncomfortable positions, especially since there were several meals that needed to be bought, and you just can't let students or adults go hungry.

The problem is that most people don't bring a lot of extra money with them so it really puts them in a bind to have to lend money. Also, they have to know that they will get that money paid back when they get home.

Unfortunately some parents at home may not be as sympathetic to their student's plight, especially if they feel their student has spent their money unwisely and then run out. This may be true, but on the other hand I've witnessed unforeseen circumstances come up with unexpected expenses, or meals just costing more than we had thought they would. Sometimes parents would not send enough money to begin with, somehow thinking their child would have enough.

I would recommend that first of all you encourage each person to bring a minimum amount of foreign money with him or her. Try to determine an estimated amount that would cover all the meals and a few souvenirs and explain to the parents that they need to send at least this amount with their student, and provide an ATM card for extra cash if needed. This can be a real learning experience for all and a chance for good, honest communication between parents and students.

In case of emergencies you do need a backup plan as a group. This entails good communication between the students, the chaperones, and the Leader of the group. Students, or adults for that matter, may be embarrassed if they lose their money, or run out, but need to know that there will be someone who will listen and help them out.

I suggest that before you leave on the trip your Committee create a plan for this. You could plan to have one person who either carries extra money with them, or has access to extra money via an ATM machine (maybe from your group's treasurer). You would have procedures in place that have been clearly explained to all the parents beforehand as to how these emergencies will be handled.

You want a student to feel comfortable to go to their chaperone and explain their situation. The two of them would then go to the person with the money and request a loan. Have the student call home as soon as possible and explain the situation to their parents and also have the chaperone explain to the parents that they were loaning the student a certain amount of money, and would expect to be paid back as soon as possible. Also have them fill out a form (that you have made up earlier) with the amount borrowed written down, the date, and the person's signature. Sometimes with the time zones and the traveling it may be impossible to call home right away, but try to call as soon as possible.

You may want to give them only enough money for meals, and have it understood that they are to spend it only on meals. Sometimes students may try to borrow from other students and adults too, for souvenirs and other items. Everyone has to decide for him or herself on this one. Nobody likes to see someone disappointed because they can't buy souvenirs, especially if it is due to unfortunate circumstances. Your group will need to discuss their policy on this, as far as the amount they are willing to loan someone and what limitations you might want to put on it.

You are taking a chance on this one, especially when you tell the whole group before you leave that you will have money available for emergencies. Sometimes parents may try to take advantage by just not sending enough money for their student and then expecting your group to take care of them. However this is not usually the case and you will be providing a great service to help those out in unfortunate circumstances. Just make it clear that any loans will need to be paid back in a timely manner and that parents will be called as soon as possible on the trip to explain the situation and secure their permission to lend the money whenever possible.

I think it is best to have a frank discussion with all the parents and students and make sure everyone understands the procedures involved. Also, encourage everyone to have backup plans for their finances (ATM cards, credit cards, extra cash), and **especially**, using a money belt. Just wearing one and keeping extra cash and cards in it will save everyone a lot of grief.

Another possible need for emergency money would be if someone gets sick and needs to pay for medications and/or treatment that they did not plan on. It is nice to be able to loan someone the cash they need in an emergency like this. This is another situation that needs to be discussed with the parents for their consideration. They need to realize that these situations could arise and that they need to be prepared.

Tips

Remember to save some for tips for your bus drivers, tour guides and the hotel maids if your stay is longer than a few days. Check with your Travel Agent about this ahead of time for the proper amounts and procedures, and be sure to let everyone know so they are prepared at the end of the trip if you need to leave tips. Hard feelings can occur if most of the people leave tips but a few claim they are all out of money, yet have lots of souvenirs, or are still buying other stuff.

Chaperones can send a ziplock bag around the bus on one of the last days of the trip indicating a suggested amount per person to be put in it. The Leader can discuss with the chaperones when the best time would be to do this.

In the United States if you stay in a hotel more than 1 day you should probably leave a tip. A dollar or two per day should suffice. Remind your students that this is per person and they need to be considerate. They can leave the tip altogether on a table or dresser the day they will be leaving.

On one trip I heard a story about a room of girls that were upset that some of their money was missing. They had left some coins on top of one of the dressers and were upset when their money was gone the next evening. The hotel maid had assumed that it was a tip!!!

Tips for meals are another consideration. Have the Travel Agent explain what are the expected amounts, if any. In some countries the tips are included in the price of the meal, or figured into the total bill. In the U.S. the customary tip is 15 to 20%.

Sometimes hotels have bellhops who may carry your luggage to your room, for a price. Remind everyone that if they use this service they need to pay for it. It is usually $1 per bag in the U.S. Occasionally your hotel may offer complimentary luggage service to carry your luggage downstairs when you are leaving. They will usually ask you to leave your bags outside your room at a designated time and they take the luggage down and put them on carts to be pushed out to your waiting buses. There would be no tip needed for this.

Remind everyone that tipping is part of being a considerate traveler and everyone needs to share in his or her part. Customs do vary from country to country so you need to find out the proper procedures before you leave.

Leftover Money

One last thing, remind all the travelers to be careful towards the end of the trip to not have too much foreign currency left when they come back home. You can change it back but it will cost you. Banks usually won't take coins back.

If you do end up with some foreign currency at the airport before you depart for home there are usually duty free shops where you might be able to pick up some nice items at good prices. Sometimes there are even "sales" on the flight back. I was so surprised on the flight back from England when they came around with a catalog of things you could buy from the flight attendants. I bought several chocolate bars!!! I would not count on this option however to get rid of your extra cash.

Foreign Money

It is really helpful when traveling in a foreign country to have some understanding of what the exchange rate is and how much the money is really worth in the United States. It is easy to spend more than you would like on something simply because you don't really know how much you are spending. It is also helpful to have some idea what the coins look like and what they are worth, and what the denominations of the bills are. If you have time I would suggest you concentrate on this in your March meeting. If possible try to have real foreign currency and coins from the countries you will be visiting for everyone to look at.

If you are traveling to more than one foreign country you may need different currencies. For example, you may fly out of Canada to England, then on to France. You should probably take some American money, some Canadian money, some English Pounds and some Euros. You can keep them straight be keeping them in separate ziplock bags. Be sure to label each bag!

A foreign currency converter chart can come in very handy. You can find them where travel supplies are sold. You may be able to print charts off the Internet too.

VAT - Value Added Tax

Many countries, especially European ones, have high sales taxes, 15 to 25 percent. Travelers can get these taxes refunded but there are a few requirements. The item usually has to cost over $100 and you have to buy it at a store that participates in the Tax-free Program. You need to get a special receipt from the store and then take it to a particular booth at the airport before you leave. They will give you a form to fill out and an envelope to return it in by mail.

My son Jon bought a leather jacket at the Hard Rock Café in London. They were very gracious in explaining the VAT refund procedure to him. Jon found the booth in the airport before we left for home and was able to get the proper forms. We mailed it when we returned home and received the refund about a month later.

Customs

If you are on an international trip, when you return to the United States you will go through Customs at the airport. You are allowed to bring

$400 worth of souvenirs back home duty-free. The next $1000 is taxed at 10 percent. Anything over that is taxed according to each individual item's rate. You will have received a Customs Declaration Form on the airplane during your flight home. You will need to fill this out and have it ready when it is your turn to go through Customs. You should have saved all your receipts from your purchases and will be able to show them if need be. If the value is over $400 you will have to pay the duty (tax) then. Be prepared to open your suitcase if asked.

Remember that everyone has to fill out his or her own Customs Declaration form, even if a parent is on the trip. Everyone goes through Customs on their own.

SHOPPING TIPS

The following are a few tips that I have learned over the years about shopping on a trip, especially in a foreign country:

- *Don't hesitate if you really love the item:* If you find something you really love, go ahead and buy it then. Don't say "I'll think about it and come back later". Chances are you won't be able to come back because you've run out of time, or you can't find the store again. I've learned the hard way several times on this one and still regret some of the things I didn't buy. However, be sure to consult your trip budget.

- *You like it but you're not sure you want to spend that much:* Consider your budget first, are you on track, or have you spent more than you have planned? Are there other stops coming up where you will want to buy a lot more souvenirs? Maybe you'll find something later that you really love, and is cheaper. Calculate what is costs in American money…this may help you decide if it is really too expensive for the value.

- *It is made in the country you are visiting or in one nearby:* You really have to think about this one. Sometimes you can get the same thing back in the States…but it's just not the same as buying it in the country where you are traveling. However, be careful to check labels carefully. I was with a group of friends in a store in Bath, England, where they had a lot of wool items marked "Made in the British Isles" and "Made in Scotland". We all got very excited and bought several items. Back on the bus a friend of mine looked at her new fleece scarf with teddy bears on it and it's label said "Made in the USA"!!!

- *You are not sure what it would cost in U.S. money:* You need to really familiarize yourself with what the exchange rate is. It can change daily, but it usually won't change too much. Think through, and even write down if you wish, what different denominations are worth in U.S. money. There are handy currency converter charts that you can get. It is so easy to look at a marked price and think that it is a really good deal, and then realize later that it actually cost 1 1/2 times that amount in U.S. money.

- *You would like to buy it but it's too big for your suitcase or you are running out of room:* Ask the store if they could ship it and how much it will cost. Then you have to determine if it is worth that to you. A German Coocoo clock may well be worth the shipping costs, while other items may not. You might be able to talk someone into carrying it in his or her suitcase for you. Some people have even bought an extra suitcase and put their extra souvenirs in that and checked it at the airport. You do need to know ahead of time if you have any limits on the amount of luggage you are allowed per person. There may be weight limits too.

Bargaining

If by chance you are going to a foreign country where you may be doing some bargaining to buy your souvenirs you might want to bring in a speaker to explain the ins and outs of bargaining. You might want the travelers to practice bargaining with one another during one of your meetings to get a "feel" for the bargaining experience. Your speaker may be able to give you an idea of what are good prices to look for and how to get them.

Bargaining can be a very fun experience, but it can also be frustrating to figure out if you are getting a good price or not. Sellers can be very persuasive and may put a lot of pressure on you. You need to be very aware of what is going on. Sometimes you will just have to look at it as a learning experience and not worry about it.

CHAPTER 8
-
MEDICAL CONCERNS

HEALTH AND SAFETY

First Aid Items

There is a lot of controversy now over students carrying medications on a high school campus. If yours is a school-sponsored trip you may have to have several discussions with school administrators to come up with a plan that is both practical for traveling yet will not cause your students any problems with the drug policies of your school district. This can be a very tricky issue so you need to consider it carefully and discuss all your options with your Committee and a school district representative.

You also need to have a discussion about the issue of liability of anyone who is going in the capacity of "nurse" or medical person with the parents. Even if these people are receiving "free trips" and especially if they are not, it needs to be made clear that they will act in a manner that they feel is best for the health of the students, and will do the best job they possibly can. However, they are not all knowing and cannot be expected to work miracles or be held liable for things beyond their control. Also, sometimes students, or adults, may choose to not follow their advice and must accept the consequences of their own behavior.

The medical person may feel it is best to consult a doctor or emergency room while on the trip, which may cause extra expenses for the parents. The parents need to understand that this is a possibility and accept the medical person's decision.

Some school districts do not like the idea of students carrying any medication with them, including prescription drugs. They may want the medical person to carry all the medication. On a trip with a large group of students this may not at all be practical. The group may be on different flights many hours apart and then be in separate tour buses throughout the trip.

Prescription medicine usually needs to be taken at specified times, and certain ones need to be carried with the person at all times (asthma inhalers, insulin, epinephrine pens). Over-the-counter medication can be needed at any time too (motion sickness pills, headache pain medication, diarrhea medication). It is extremely impractical to ask one person to have to carry all this medication and be responsible for handing it out to a large group of students.

Hopefully you will be able to work out some kind of arrangement with the school district to allow all the students to carry their own prescription medicine and any over-the-counter medication that they think they might need. You might need to have some sort of form that parents fill out and sign indicating the prescription and over-the-counter medication that students will be carrying on the trip and declaring their permission for the student to take as directed or needed. A doctor's signature may be needed for the prescription medicine if the school district insists.

Regardless of what the school district says, every traveler needs to have a form listing all prescription drugs and over-the-counter medication that they are carrying with them along with an explanation of any specific conditions they are treating. This information should be a part of every person's medical history, and carried with him or her at all times. If there were to be some sort of accident or illness this information will be extremely helpful to have at hand. The nurse/medical person should also carry a copy of this information, and possibly the assigned chaperone too. It is my personal opinion that every traveler, student and adult, needs to carry his or her own personal "*Traveler's First Aid Kit*" too. This kit would include:

- any prescription medicine that you are taking, especially asthma inhalers and an epinephrine pen if you have severe allergies to peanuts, bee stings
- an assortment of band-aids
- antiseptic handiwipes
- antibiotic ointment
- moleskin
- pain reliever (acetaminophen, ibuprofen)
- medication for upset stomach and/or diarrhea; antacid
- cold and cough medication (Sudafed, Benadryl)
- medicated sore throat lozenges
- tiny salt packages that you get at Wendy's or McDonald's (work great for gargling a sore throat)
- motion sickness medication if needed
- sunscreen, lip balm, after sun moisturizer, aloe vera gel
- an ace bandage, knee wrap or brace if you know you have problems in this area

When I was on a trip with 8th graders I hurt my knee stepping off a curb at Arlington Cemetery. I used an ace bandage from the buses' first aid kit until I was able to buy a knee wrap at a drug store (which was no easy thing to find with the busy schedule). My knee did not bother me again until another trip with a lot of walking. Sometimes you just don't know what will happen but you need to try to be as prepared as possible.

If anyone is taking prescription medicine remind him or her to make sure they take enough of the medicine with them. It can be very difficult to fill prescriptions in some countries, if not impossible. People using asthma inhalers should take at least 2 and ideally 3 inhalers with them in case 1 or 2 of them don't work. They should have one with them at all times, and one in their carry-on bag, and another in their checked baggage.

Remind your students' parents that their students need to have their own medications. They should not expect a chaperone to give their student over-the-counter medications. It always amazes me that some parents just expect the chaperones and/or nurse to provide medications for their children. If a parent knows that their son or daughter is prone to headaches, motion sickness, sore knees, sensitive stomachs, they need to plan accordingly and talk with their student about these concerns as well as other medical situations that may arise and send medications for them. It would also be a good idea to discuss their concerns with the chaperone assigned to their student and the nurse/medical person.

We will discuss traveling health specifically later in this chapter, but it is a good idea to start assembling the "Traveler's First Aid Kit" as soon as possible, since it involves a certain amount of expense. Try to find the smallest packages the over-the-counter medication comes in. The foil wrapped individual dosages are very handy, but can be expensive. You probably won't need just one Tylenol. All your medications need to be in their labeled, original containers. You may need to ask the druggist for a smaller container. This may save you lots of hassles if you are searched at the airport. Don't have a bag of loose pills that only you know what they are! You can put all your first aid supplies in a zip-lock bag to be carried in your carry-on bag. You might want to put a few band-aids, pain reliever, along with any prescription drugs that you need during the day in a small zip-lock bag to be carried in your daypack too. Don't forget a small bottle of vitamins if you are currently taking them. You don't want to upset your regular routine, and you want to give your health a boost.

Extra Supplies

Someone on the trip should always carry some extra First Aid supplies. The logical person would be a nurse/medical person if you are lucky enough to have one. Otherwise another designated person should carry a few extra items. The supplies should include:

- Thermometer w/protective covers
- Tweezers
- Scissors
- Moleskin
- Extra bandages
- Gauze, Telfa pads
- Medical tape
- Ace bandages
- 2-3 disposable ice packs
- Baking soda for bee stings
- Small bottle of hydrogen peroxide
- Alcohol pads
- Antiseptic ointment
- Several pairs of rubber gloves
- 1st Aid Book

Vaccinations

You will need to check with your Travel Agent if any specific vaccinations are needed for the countries you will be visiting. It would be a good idea if everyone knows when he or she had their last tetanus shot. If it has been more than 10 years they should get a booster shot.

Medical Forms

Before you leave on the trip you will need to have every traveler fill out a Medical History and Medical Release and Consent to Treat Form. The parents need to sign these for their students so that you will have permission to take them to a doctor and/or hospital to obtain medical treatment. All adults should fill out this form also because they may get sick or hurt too. There also may be a Prescription Drug Form that will need to be filled out if anybody is taking any prescriptions drugs. This may need to be signed by a doctor.

If you have a "Field Trip Permission Form" from each student it may have a "permission to treat" area on it. However, I think it is good to have a separate form with the Medical History on it too, along with the Medical Release and Consent to Treat statement. This form should also have an area for Medical Insurance information on it.

The Medical History doesn't need to be really long but just have any major health concerns listed on it, any allergies, especially to any drugs and a list of ALL medications currently being taken, prescription and over-the-counter. The date of the last tetanus shot is very important too.

After filling out one of these medical histories it would be helpful to put the same information on an index card and carry it in your money belt so you will have your medical history with you at all times. Your doctor's name and phone number, as well as your insurance carrier and phone number should be on this too.

Your School District may request that each student have a Prescription Drug Form signed by a parent and/or doctor listing any prescription medications they are taking, including the dosages and times for taking. Be sure to check with them. If a student is taking a controlled substance such as Ritalin, Aderol, or a similar drug that may be used to treat Attention Deficit Disorder you will want to have a letter from the doctor explaining the prescription.

As with all prescription drugs and over-the-counter medication as well, they should ALWAYS be in the original container.

The Leader of the group should carry the Medical/Consent Forms and the Field Trip Permission Forms with him/her at all times. If your group is traveling in more than one bus there should be a set of all forms on each bus carried by the chaperones assigned to that particular bus.

If you have a nurse/medical person traveling with your group in the capacity as "Trip Nurse/Medical Person" that person will also need a full set of these forms and will be expected to carry the forms with them all of the time. You may want each chaperone to carry a copy of the Medical/Consent Forms for the students they are chaperoning also. Adults may want to ask another adult to carry a copy of their form.

Amusement Parks

If your group will be visiting an amusement park where everyone will be scattering all over the park for several hours you will need an additional set of these forms. These types of parks usually ask that the Leader check in at the "First Aid Station" and leave a set of medical forms there. When it is time to leave the park the Leader picks up the forms. It is a good idea to have a spare set of forms for these kinds of situations because you do not want to accidentally leave your only set of forms there.

You will need to set up a system for someone to check back at the First Aid Station every hour or so to see if someone in the group has become ill or hurt. This would most likely be the nurse/medical person and/or the chaperones. To relieve the nurse/medical person somewhat you could have he or she check back every three hours or so and have chaperones check every hour.

Most amusement parks will have phones throughout the park that you can call the First Aid Station with. You give them your group's name and ask if anyone is there from your group.

In any case, if someone is at the First Aid Station an adult will need to go to the station and check on the person. Since everyone needs to stay in at least groups of two remind students and adults not to go off and leave someone by themselves in these situations.

Once the chaperones and/or medical person have checked at the Station they will need to decide what needs to be done. Usually it will be something simple: headache, blister, mild case of dehydration. First Aid Stations are not usually set up for people to stay there very long. Hopefully the person will be feeling better by the time someone gets there.

If it is really serious the park may insist upon transporting them to the hospital. Hopefully the nurse/chaperone will be able to contact the Leader of the group and discuss the situation with them and they will be able to decide what will need to be done.

A group may have a set or two of the "talk about" mini walkie-talkies. They can have the Leader, medical person and maybe some of the chaperones carry them to keep in touch. That way the medical person can notify the Leader if a student is sick or hurt.

Cell phones may work well in these situations too, provided you have local coverage. Everyone needs to know the numbers to call too.

If someone needs to be transported to a hospital an adult will need to go with him or her. Then they will need to arrange for transportation back to the housing site. Be sure everyone knows the name of the housing site!

MEDICAL RELEASE FORM

The following is a suggested Medical Release Form. This would work well for students as well as adults. The forms should be collected, copied, and alphabetized for ease in finding the individual forms. You might want to separate the adults from the students. You will need several copies of these forms and keep them in separate folders. The Leader needs one set for him or her, another set to use at amusement parks, if needed. The nurse/medical person will need a set too. There should also be one full set on each bus. A full set is needed because there may be changes during the trip of who is on each bus, so it is easier to have a full set on each bus.

Chaperones may want to keep an up to date list of who is on each bus too. Each assigned chaperone should have a copy of each of their assigned students' Medical Release Form too, and chaperones should carry copies of each other's forms. The Leader should have a copy of each adult's also.

If someone has extensive medical conditions or concerns they should attach additional pages with the conditions described and treatments and/or medications that they are taking explained in more depth.

A full size copy of this form is found in the Appendix too. When you collect these forms be sure that they are completely filled out. This information is extremely important.

MEDICAL RELEASE FORM

Name________________________Date of Birth__________Age_____
Student Adult

Address____

Parent/Legal Guardian______________________Phone #___________

EMERGENCY TELEPHONE NUMBERS
Work Phone:
(Father)__________________(Mother)__________________
Emergency contact:
(1)_____________________(2)_______________________
(Name & Phone #) (Name & Phone #)

MEDICAL INFORMATION
Prescription medication student must take on trip:_________________

Other medication student must take on trip:______________________

Over-the-counter medication that student has parent permission to carry on trip and to take as needed. Parent has discussed with student dosage and indications where medication might be needed:_______________
____

Allergies to food, medications, bee stings, etc._________________
Date of last tetanus shot:__________________

Pertinent medical history and/or any chronic medical problems:____

____

MEDICAL INSURANCE
Medical Insurance Carrier:______________________________

Name of Insured:___________________Policy Number:____________

MEDICAL RELEASE
In case of emergency and a parent cannot be reached by telephone, or I am incapacitated, I authorize the leader of this event, or his/her designee, to obtain medical treatment for my son/daughter, or myself, as needed. I also give permission for any hospital emergency department physician and/or member of the hospital medical staff requested by this physician to make examinations and provide medical and/or surgical treatment which in his or their judgement may be deemed necessary for my child's, or my own health and welfare.

Signature________________________Signature________________
(Parent/Guardian; Adult) (Student)

FEELING GOOD, OR NOT, DURING YOUR TRIP

Feeling good on a trip is not an impossibility but it does take some planning and some self-discipline. To begin with, you must be kind to your body before the trip even starts. During the week before your departure date you really need to get lots of extra rest and be drinking lots of water. This may seem really simple but usually the time before your trip will be a pretty hectic time in your life while you are busy getting ready for the trip plus taking care of all your other responsibilities. For students it will probably be a busy time with tests and projects due, and possibly extra school work too, because of missing a few days of classes as well.

If you will be having a performance before the trip it should be at least two weeks before you leave on the trip. You will then have plenty of time to get your performance clothes ready for the trip as well as preparing the instruments and other needed items for traveling. This will also help make the week before your trip less hectic.

My suggestion is that travelers look at their schedules for the two weeks before the trip and see how they can "lighten the load" for the week before you leave. Try to get extra sleep during that week because you probably will be so excited the night before the trip that you might not be able to sleep anyway, or at least not much.

Drinking lots of water and other beverages, but not heavily caffeine laden ones, the week before is really important. Caffeine is dehydrating but most will not be able to be without at least a few cups of coffee or pop every day. Just make sure you drink lots of water too. Plane flights and tour buses have extremely dry air so you want to start out well hydrated.

If you are starting to feel sick before your trip begins you will want to check with your doctor. This is especially true if you are getting all congested in your sinuses. Congestion is miserable on airplane flights. Your doctor may prescribe a decongestant for you, or you may get by with an over-the-counter one. However, decongestants usually make you very sleepy. If you want to avoid this you may want to try a nasal decongestant spray one half-hour before you board the plane. Do check with your doctor for advice.

Getting sick during a trip is no fun for anyone but is especially difficult when you are traveling with students. Most students still rely on their parents to "nurse" them through illnesses, no matter how small, and to remind them to take care of themselves. On a trip like this most of the students' parents will not be with you so the chaperones and hopefully a nurse/medical person that is traveling with you will need to assume the role of parent and watch out for any illnesses.

This is a good reason for the chaperones to get to know the students and their parents before the trip starts. That way the parents can talk with their students' chaperones and share with them any health concerns their students may have. The chaperones should be familiar with the health history of the students they are chaperoning too so they will have a better understanding of them, and better able to be of assistance if needed. However, this should be confidential with the chaperone, medical person, and the Leader.

This is also a good time for the parents to talk to their students about taking care of themselves and self-medicating if needed. Just talking about when to take a pain reliever or upset stomach medicine can help a lot. Most students should be able to handle minor problems just fine. However, they need to be encouraged to share any health concerns they have on the trip with their chaperone. They need to know that they will be listened to and if there is a problem they may have to talk to the nurse/medical person if there is one or that something else may need to be done.

It is really important to talk about this and to make every effort to keep the lines of communication open. On one of the trips I was on we had an unfortunate incident where a student did not share with the chaperones how sick she was becoming. By the time the adults found out she was in really bad shape.

Even though chaperones may feel really bad that a student is not feeling well and may be very tempted to give them a pain reliever or other medication, **they should not give a student medication.** A chaperone should not take the risk of giving medication, no matter how well intentioned, because of the chance of allergic reactions or other problems.

A call home to discuss the situation with parents may help alleviate some of the concerns. A parent may give permission for the chaperone/medical person to buy and/or give over-the-counter medication if needed though this situation needs to be thoroughly discussed.

If a student's illness is beyond being able to be taken care of by his or her own self-medication and/or discussion with the nurse it may be time to visit an emergency room at a hospital. The Travel Agent and/or the hotel you are staying at may be able to direct you to the closest one.

When I went to Mexico on a band trip with my two older sons, my son James started not feeling well on the flight there. He had a slight sore throat and felt a little feverish and achy. The only thing I could do for him was give him ibuprofen and tell him to drink a lot of water. I also encouraged him to gargle with salt water, but it was a little difficult to find salt and we could only drink bottled water so the water was not very warm to gargle with.

He felt progressively worse as the trip went on and I felt that there was not much that I could do to help him. I was very uneasy about contacting a doctor there. When we were in Acapulco I saw a sign saying there was an English-speaking doctor available at a hotel but by that time he was starting to feel a little better. I was able to buy some throat lozenges there, the first time I had found any on the whole trip. He was able to get around, he just didn't feel at 100 %.

As soon as we returned home from the trip we took him to the doctor to get him checked out just in case. He did have a nasty throat infection and it took time for him to get over it.

I still think back and wonder if I made the right decision about not taking him to a doctor in Mexico. It is hard to know about another country's medical facilities so each person has to decide for him or herself. However, when you are responsible for someone else's child you really need to think about the situation very carefully. If James had been someone else's child I probably would have taken them to the doctor if I had felt confident in the medical facilities. We were in Mexico and I was unsure of their medical facilities. I have felt much more confidant in England and in the United States with the available medical facilities.

Also you need to decide how sick they really are. With my son James I didn't think he was sick enough to need a doctor. In my experiences on the various trips and activities I have been on with students they could usually take care of themselves with their own medication. There were times however when we had to take students to emergency rooms. Cuts, sprained wrists, asthma problems, dehydration, diabetic reactions, have resulted in visits to emergency rooms. Consent to Treat Forms helped things go very smoothly. It also helps for people to have an insurance card with them too. These numbers must be on the Consent to Treat Forms as well, though the card seems to help things go a little quicker. Parents are usually called as soon as possible, although sometimes you may be unable to get in contact with them right away.

The cost needs to be considered too. Usually insurance will cover most of the costs. However, in some countries they will expect payment from the patient at the time of service and the patient will then need to submit the bills to their insurance company for reimbursement. Any prescriptions that are needed will usually have to be paid for at the time of dispensing. Unfortunately most students will not have brought enough extra money to pay for medications and/or treatment. Your group might want to arrange to have access to a certain amount of money to pay for such emergencies. In a situation like this you will have probably called the parents anyway so you will have to explain the cost of the medications and get their assurance that they will pay your group back when you all return from the trip. If treatment needs to be paid for at the time of service the parents will need to be contacted first and they will need to arrange for payment with the hospital.

I was on a trip to Florida and one of the boys smashed his finger in the luggage compartment of the bus. Our nurse took him to the emergency room where they took care of it and the expenses were covered by his insurance. But he did need a prescription for antibiotics and the chaperones had to pay for this since he had very little money. After that we decided to take extra money on trips, or at least have access to some through an ATM card.

Trip Medical Insurance needs to be considered very carefully, especially if the trip involves countries with questionable medical facilities. Purchasing this insurance usually provides for medical evacuation if needed due to injury or extreme illness. If illness or an accident happens to a traveler while in a foreign country this type of insurance may be a lifesaver, as well as protecting your life's savings.

Another thing your group needs to discuss before you leave on the trip is what to do if someone is not feeling well during the trip. If you are staying at the same place for awhile this is a lot easier to deal with. If they need to stay at the housing site instead of participating in the day's activities an adult needs to stay with them and check on them several times during the day. Usually this person would be the nurse/medical person, since they are probably receiving a "free trip" and are the logical one to miss the day's events. However, this does leave the group without a medical person during that time.

Sometimes another chaperone will not mind staying back with an ill student. They actually might like to get a little more rest and enjoy the slower pace for awhile. Good communication among the chaperones can really help in situations like this.

If you are moving from place to place it is a lot more difficult to deal with an ill traveler. You can only hope that they will be able to handle all the traveling. They may need to stay on the bus while the rest of the group participates in the scheduled activities. An adult will need to stay with them too. Ideally there would be 2 adults staying back.

Hints to help you feel better:

- The best advice I've ever heard for travelers is: "If you can sit down, don't stand; if you can lay down, don't sit; if you get a chance to eat

- and drink, take it, you never know for sure when your next meal will be; if you have a restroom break, take it!"

- Drink as much water and other beverages on the flights as possible. Try to avoid a lot of beverages with caffeine. If you start feeling queasy on a flight you might want to ask for some Ginger Ale. Ginger cookies can help on a bus trip sometimes. Motion sickness medicine works but it can make you very sleepy too.

- Chewing gum and sucking on hard candy can help a lot with dry throats, so make sure you take plenty with you and use them on the flights and the bus rides.

- Be sure your walking shoes are well broken in before you leave but you should bring moleskin and band-aids anyway. You may still get blisters from all the extra walking you will be doing. Shoe insole inserts are nice to put in your shoes for extra comfort. Your feet may swell a lot more than you might expect. Putting your feet up for a little while in the afternoon can help this a lot.

- Wash your hands as often as you can but especially before eating. If this is impossible try one of the antibacterial waterless gel cleansers.

- Sometimes you may start feeling a little sick: headache, queasy, shaky, and you are just dehydrated. You can become dehydrated very quickly in hot weather, but even when it is cool, it is easy to become dehydrated from flying on an airplane and traveling on buses, where the air can be very dry. Always carry a bottle of water with you and don't forget to drink. Juices and sports drinks can be helpful too, though sometimes the high sugar content can make you nauseous.

    - A word of caution here: sometimes you may find yourself sensitive to the local water (diarrhea, nausea). It is not that the water is bad, but each area's water has certain characteristics and you may be sensitive to some of them. If you feel this might be the case with you be sure to drink bottled water.

- If you are going somewhere that you will be exposed to the sun be sure to apply lots of sunscreen, and keep reapplying it often. It is easy to get sunburned very quickly, especially if you are not used to being out in the sun. Even if it is partly cloudy you can still get sunburned when you are out walking around. If you do get sunburned apply some sort of aloe vera lotion to help relieve the pain and speed up healing. Be sure to check with your doctor if you are taking any prescriptions that may cause you to be sensitive to the sun.

- Sunlight is wonderful for jet lag, so be out in it as much as possible.

SAFETY

A big issue on your trip should be personal safety. Most safety problems can be avoided by **always** being in a group, or at least with one other person, **all of the time.** Even if you are just going to the restroom in a museum you still need to have at least one other person with you, standing outside the door if need be.

You should also **always** have a copy of your itinerary with you everywhere you go. This is in case you get separated from the group. You will at least then know where the next stop is or where the housing is for that night along with pertinent phone numbers.

It is very helpful to write down the address or street names where the bus will be to pick you up. It is easy to get confused when you are touring a town and you may not be able to figure out how to get back to where you need to be. If you have an address you can probably ask a local to direct you how to get there.

It is not a good idea to accept a ride from just anyone. You may need to take a taxi if you cannot find where you need to be.

There should be some discussion with the whole travel group as to the procedures to follow if some of the group does get lost. The buses may be instructed to wait a certain length of time and then proceed to the next stop. This is a very difficult decision to make, especially if someone is missing. The Leader will need to decide the appropriate action to take. Some may need to stay at the designated meeting spot to wait for the missing members, with the understanding that someone will be returning for them at a certain time. The lost travelers may be instructed to return to the pick up spot if possible, and then proceed to the next stop by taxi if no one is there.

Lost travelers can also be encouraged to call the housing site for that night to leave a message as to where they are. The telephone numbers of all the housing sites should be printed on the itinerary.

Students need to be reminded too that it is OK to talk to the locals but they should not go anywhere with anyone they do not know. However, if they are with a group (more than two) of their friends they could meet a group of locals for coffee or even a meal as long as they stay in public places and keep their wits about them. While there is safety in numbers everyone needs to remember to be aware of their surroundings.

They should also avoid telling anyone they meet where their housing site is for that night. They really don't need visitors showing up unless they have checked with the Leader of the group about a special situation.

If the group is carrying cell phones then lost travelers can simply call the numbers of the Leader or others to let them know where they are. These numbers should also be printed on the itinerary, and possibly another card to be carried in the wallet or money belt.

If lost travelers are feeling very uneasy about where they are they need to look for local police authorities and ask them for help.

While traveling in a foreign country where another language is spoken be sure everyone has his or her foreign language translation book with him or her. Being lost and unable to speak the language can be very frightening. However, a lot of people do speak English in other countries too, so you may be able to make yourself understood.

We have already discussed keeping track of possessions but here are a few more hints:

- Always keep track of your money belt. When you take it off at night put it in a safe place, possibly locked in your suitcase.
- If you use a communal bathroom, such as in a hostel, you may need to take turns with a friend, with one of you staying with your stuff while the other showers. This is especially important if you are sharing a room with others that you do not know.
- Keep your wallet, with only the day's cash in it, in an inside pocket, on your person.
- While using a public restroom hang your daypack on a hook on the door if possible. If there is no hook keep it between your legs, not on the edge of the stall where someone might reach in and grab it.

If passports, money, credit cards are lost or stolen you will need to report this to the local police authorities, especially if the items are stolen. Lost passports will need to be reported to the nearest American Embassy. They will help with getting replacements. Copies of the passport identification page will make the replacement process go much more quickly and easily. If your Travel Agent is traveling with you he or she should be able to help you with this.

You will need to call credit card companies and banks as soon as possible so the account numbers can be cancelled and you will not have to pay for purchases made by someone else.

CHAPTER 9

-

PACKING

PACKING SUGGESTIONS

The key to packing well is to pack as light as possible while bringing the necessities and still having room for souvenirs. When you are traveling with a group of students you may not have the freedom to go shopping for extra clothes or items you forgot or you run out of. You most likely will need to stay with the group and your itinerary may not have this kind of shopping in it. Sometimes housing sites will have toiletries available for purchase, or you may be near a drug store, or you may not. It is fun to buy items in a foreign country that you may need; though you may not want to spend your souvenir money on shampoo. When we were in England I had fun buying "plasters" when I was running low on Band-Aids.

If you are using travel sized items you may want to try using a whole travel sized shampoo, toothpaste, mouthwash, up while at home to see how long it will last you. If it appears that you will run out of travel sized shampoo you can always take two travel sizes and throw away the one when you use it up. Don't take full sized bottles, you won't need that much, unless your trip is more than two weeks or so, and they weigh too much and take up a lot of space. If you can't find travel sizes in your brands you can buy small squeeze bottles and put your brands in them. Be sure to put any bottles in ziplock bags. Pressure changes can cause lids to blow off bottles.

Uses for Ziplock Bags:

- *Snack size:* vitamins (labeled), small contact lens case and bottle of solution, packets of Tylenol , toothpaste, gum, hard candy, ear plugs, jewelry, q-tips, cotton balls, currency and coins (sorted by country), information card (phone #'s) in money belt

- *Sandwich size:* tissues, toilet paper, soap, travel size shampoo, deck of cards, anti-bacterial cleanser, nail polish and nail polish remover pads, crayons, bandaids

- *Quart size:* manicure supplies, mouthwash, feminine supplies, snacks: granola bars, cookies, notepad, pen, film, exposed film, sunscreen, washcloth, ice, First Aid supplies, medications

- *Gallon size:* journal, water bottle, contact lens supplies if larger bottles

- *Two-Gallon size:* underwear, socks, swimsuit, towel, clothes

Carry-On Bags

A properly packed carry-on bag can help make your trip a very enjoyable one, but an improperly packed one can cause you lots of problems. The first things to find out are the dimensions and weight that the airline allows. Usually for a carry-on they are 14" X 22" X 8" with a maximum weight of thirteen pounds. Please be advised that they are not kidding about these restrictions. Airlines will usually have a "bin" that you can put your bag in to see if it fits these dimensions. You should also weigh your bag to make sure it is well under the weight limit. Remember you may have more souvenirs and other items when you come back. Airlines do not want heavy bags in overhead storage bins because they may fall out during turbulence and hurt someone.

When we were at the airport in England, ready to return home, a flight attendant was standing on the walkway to the plane and picked up the carry-on bag I was carrying to see if it weighed too much. It felt really heavy to me, it was full of souvenirs, especially books, but she said it was OK. My friend was not so lucky. She said the flight attendant told her that her carry-on was too heavy and she would have to take some of the items out and ask others to carry them in their bags. Luckily she was able to find a few students to carry some of her things.

The carry-on bag also needs a luggage tag with the owner's name and address on it as well as a card inside the bag with the same name, address and phone number on it. There should be some other identifying mark on the bag: brightly colored yarn or fabric tied on the handle, large stickers on the bag, large brightly colored luggage tag, that the owner can easily spot. Luggage locks are a good idea. Be sure you have the keys with you, maybe hidden on a key chain in an outside pocket of the carry-on so you can easily get to it. Carry two keys but on separate key chains in separate places, maybe one in your wallet or money belt.

There are two main reasons for having a carry-on bag. One is to carry the items you will need on the trip for comfort and to keep you busy. The other is to have the items that you will absolutely need for a few days on your trip if by some twist of fate your checked luggage does not arrive with you at your destination.

You will need to make this crystal clear to your students because they usually think that a carry-on is to hold items to eat and keep them busy while they are traveling. They won't even think about their checked bag not arriving with them.

Checked bags sometimes DO NOT arrive at the destination when the traveler does. On the England trip I was on one student's (out of 130) luggage did not. Since we were on the move, going from city to city, it took a few days for the bag to catch up to us. This was not fun for him. Another friend went to Japan and her bag didn't arrive for two days.

I am taking for granted that you are wearing comfortable traveling clothes, layered with an overshirt, sweater or jacket, plus a coat or jacket with a hood and/or hat if you want. You also have on a money belt with your money and other travel documents, and are carrying a wallet with only the day's spending money and your Picture Identification and other necessary items if you need them that day. You should also be wearing a watch and synchronize times with all the other travelers in your group. Women might be able to carry a small purse if they want.

One thing to think about when you are gathering all the items you want to take on the trip is if you are willing to part with that particular item if it is lost or stolen. Some items may mean more to you than other items, either sentimentally, or maybe they are worth a lot of money. You may not want to take certain items of clothing, jewelry, CD's, because you won't want to risk having them lost or stolen. Things do happen on trips, and items get lost, stolen or broken. If there are some items you can't bear for this to happen to then you need to not take them with you on the trip.

What to Put in the Carry-On:

- Have at least one full change of clothes, especially underwear and socks, and maybe something to sleep in, packed in the bag
- Toiletries in a bag or ziplock bag (soap or body wash, deodorant, shampoo/conditioner, toothpaste, toothbrush, floss, mouthwash, razor)
- Cosmetics in bag or ziplock bag (face cleanser, moisturizer, make-up, q-tips, cotton balls)
- Brush, comb, styling products, mirror
- Hair dryer, curling iron if you can't be without
- Electrical converter, travel clock
- First aid supplies (see list) and any prescription drugs and over-the-counter drugs that you might need
    - *Ziplock bag with a few bandaids, prescription drugs and over-the counter drugs that you might need on the plane
- *Tissues, lip balm, lotion, anti-bacterial gel cleanser (works great when you can't wash your hands)

- *Women: feminine protection supplies (unless you are absolutely sure you won't need them, trips have a way bringing on periods; foil wrapped cleansing pads are great for long plane rides and long sightseeing days)
- *Small amount of toilet paper in ziplock bag
- *Contact lens supplies and case (sometimes the dry air makes it difficult to wear them on a plane); spare glasses and sunglasses
- *Camera, film, extra batteries, case, ziplock bags for exposed film
- *Trip folder, magazine, book to read, small Bible, picture of family
- *Pen, pencil, notepad, journal (blank book to write down trip experiences; include an envelope to hold ticket stubs and other memorabilia); address book, Palm Pilot
- *Things to keep busy with: deck of cards, video games, coloring book, crayons
- *CD Player and CD's, extra batteries (try to take a minimum amount of CD's, you probably won't have a lot of time to listen to them anyway, and if they get lost or stolen you may be out a lot of money to replace them)
- *Bottle of water and snacks (trail mix, granola bars, cheese & crackers, candy, cookies, Pringles, nuts)
- *Gum, hard candy, breath mints
- Luggage keys
- *Ear plugs, sleep mask, small inflatable neck pillow (great for sleeping on the airplane
- Small flashlight
- Small umbrella (optional)

* Items to put in Daypack or tote bag

Travelers need to remember that once that carry-on bag is put in an overhead storage bin they should not get into it again during the flight. It can be dangerous to open overhead storage bins in-flight. Also, if there is a lot of turbulence the seatbelt light may be on a lot of the time and everyone will need to stay in his or her seats.

One way to handle this is to have a daypack or tote bag with snacks, water and items to keep you busy in it. Don't forget your camera if you want to take pictures on the plane. Put this under your seat so it is easy to get to. You should be able to put the daypack in your carry-on bag before you board the plane and then take it out when you find your seat on the plane. Put the carry-on in the storage bin and the daypack under your seat. The airline may want you to have only one carry-on to begin with so putting the daypack in the carry-on will be necessary. However, if your daypack isn't too big you might be able to bring it on separately. Check with your Travel Agent and maybe the airline.

My son Jon did this on the England trip and it worked very well for him. He had a rolling upright carry-on bag with his daypack inside.

With all of the terrorist concerns now there are certain things that should not be in your carry-on bag. If you do have them and your bag is searched at the airport you will be asked to give them up. If there is any question in your mind about an item it is better to put it in your checked bag so you won't have to worry about having to give it up. Don't try to sneak anything by the metal detector either. Things to consider putting in your checked bag are tweezers, nail files, manicure scissors, Swiss Army knives, nail clippers, razors. Put any of these that you want to take on the trip in your checked bag.

Think about any souvenirs you may buy too. When we were in England a lot of people bought beautiful letter openers decorated like swords. These would not be permitted in carry-ons now. Neither would any replica weapons. Just put them in your checked bag before you leave for the airport.

General Packing Suggestions for Your Suitcase

There are several things you can get that will help immensely in your packing. Ziplock bags in snack, sandwich, quart, gallon and two-gallon sizes are very helpful. Plastic bags from grocery or drug stores are very useful too. Lightweight cardboard or tagboard cut to fit inside your suitcase makes a convenient "shelf" to put between your clothes. This really helps in organizing and keeping wrinkles to a minimum.

Don't forget to take a few hangers and a laundry bag. The laundry bag is usually only for underwear and socks. Otherwise you will not be able to fit the bag back into the suitcase if you put other dirty clothes in it. All other dirty clothes needed to be folded or rolled up and put in the bottom of the suitcase. The laundry bag can go on top of the ziplock bags of underwear and socks.

You will need to find out from your Travel Agent if you will need to bring towels and soap. Usually hostels do not provide towels or soap. Most hotels will provide these but there may be only one towel and one washcloth per person. A lot of people prefer another towel to dry their hair with and another washcloth for their face. You will need to make a decision on this before you go. If you do take a towel and/or washcloth take an old one you wouldn't mind leaving behind and the thinner the better so it will dry faster. A hand towel may work to dry hair, instead of taking another large bath towel. If you run out of room (souvenirs can take up a lot of room) when you are ready to fly home you may want to leave the towel(s), washcloth, behind. A friend of mine did this on the way home from England so she would have room for more souvenirs.

Bring a plastic garbage bag to put your towel in if it is still wet when you have to pack to go on to another destination. If you have an outside pocket on your suitcase you may want to store it there. If it will need to be packed inside your suitcase use a large ziplock bag to make it as airtight as possible. Any kind of dampness will spread throughout all your clothes and cause you lots of problems with wrinkles.

I would suggest that on the Saturday before you are going to leave on your trip (even if you are leaving the following Thursday or Friday) you begin your packing. Hopefully you have been gathering the items you were planning on taking, and possibly have your carry-on all ready to go from the previous meeting suggestions. Be sure to allow yourself enough time to pack. Most people underestimate the amount of time it will take them to pack and then feel very rushed. Packing is very tiring too.

First of all, make sure all of the clothes you are planning on taking are washed and completely dry. Have all the clothes and other items to go in your suitcase, carry-on, and daypack, laid out in front of you. If there are any clothing restrictions or suggestions from your Leader consider all of your clothing choices and made sure they conform to the guidelines before you pack something you won't be able to wear.

Consult the packing lists and begin checking off items as you pack them. Have an itinerary in front of you and make notes as to which outfit of clothes you plan on wearing each day. Be sure to write down when you might need performance clothes or any other special changes of clothes (swimsuit, nice outfit for the theatre or special dinner). I've found this to be immensely helpful after a very tiring day when I'm not even sure which day it is. It is easy then to just look at the itinerary and get out the clothes for the next day and not even have to think about it. You may or may not want to include the outfit, underwear and socks that you have packed in your carry-on in your itinerary plan.

Something you might want to do is to make lists of all of the items in your carry-on and in your suitcase. Keep these lists in the opposite bags (carry-on list in the suitcase). This will be very helpful if your luggage is lost. Sometimes it is hard to remember what all was in the bag when you are filling out a lost luggage claim and need to write down every item and it's value.

It is a good idea to have lists of all the items you are taking in each of your bags at home too, just in case you have to fill out a claim for lost luggage at the end of your trip. Another suggestion would be to lay out all the things you are packing and take pictures of them. Don't forget the luggage too! If you have a date imprint feature on your camera be sure to use it when doing this. Try to use a camera that you won't be taking on the trip, or at least use up that role of film before you depart and leave it at home. You don't want to lose that camera and/or film too! Having pictures will help you remember what you took and you will have another way to prove that you took the items you are claiming. It will still be a hassle because you may need receipts to claim the value of the items, or some way of estimating the value.

You might want to take pictures of souvenirs that you buy during your trip just in case your luggage is lost on the return trip too.

Check your suitcase and make sure you have a luggage tag (correctly filled out), an identifying mark (thick yarn, fabric, ribbon tied on handle, sticker), luggage lock (2 keys stored separately where you know where they are). Also have an envelope inside your suitcase with a card with your name, address and phone number on it inside and a copy of your Passport page in it too. This is in case your luggage tag is ripped off and your luggage is lost. Hopefully the airline will open it, find your name and address and can then return it to you).

You can put your underwear and socks, separately, in two-gallon size ziplock bags. This helps keep them organized and together. Roll pants up if possible, or fold carefully. Shirts and tops can be laid out on top of each other or folded carefully. Be sure to pack the clothes you need first on top, then try to pack the others in the order you plan on wearing them. Some people like to put tissue paper between the layers. Pieces of tagboard cut to fit can be put halfway down a stack of clothes. Tagboard can also be used to separate dirty clothes from clean ones.

Shoes can be put in plastic store shopping bags to protect your clothes. Don't forget bags for sandals and slippers if you take them.

If you have to take performance clothes try to keep them all together in a garment bag. If you have small items: socks, bow ties, sashes, put them in ziplock bags inside the garment bag. Make sure your name is on the garment bag and the ziplock bag, with a color-coded tag if you are using them.

Be sure to put in extra plastic bags and ziplock bags of all sizes. They take up very little room and can be very useful.

If you are taking any other items be sure they are packed securely and in waterproof bags if they contain liquid.

Adjust the straps inside your suitcase to hold everything securely in place. Hopefully you will have a little extra room for those souvenirs you will be bringing back.

You really do want to pack as lightly as possible yet still have all the things you will need. If there are any hanging straps on your checked baggage be sure to take them off and put them inside the bag before you get to the airport (unless you need them for carrying the luggage). The airline will ask you to remove the straps before the baggage is checked to avoid getting them caught in their baggage equipment.

You should get all of this packing done on Saturday so that you will have Sunday to get anything you might have realized that you need after you have finished packing. You may realize that some of your clothes just aren't going to work and you will have to get some more.

Hopefully everything will fit and you will have room to spare for all those souvenirs. If for some unfortunate reason you find that your luggage is not going to work: too small, seams ripped, too heavy for you to manage, you will have a little time to figure out alternatives.

This extra time will give you a few days to think about what you have packed and to decide if you have forgotten anything or maybe that you can get by without something and can take it out of your suitcase or carry-on.

If there are items and/or clothes that you will need for the days before you leave on the trip "trial pack" them on Saturday, then take them out and use them as needed. Make a list of these items so you will be sure to put them in on departure day or the night before you leave. This is really important because it is very easy to forget things if you are using them on the days before you leave on the trip.

If there are any clothes you need to wash before you pack be sure they are thoroughly dry before you put them in your luggage. Don't wait to wash them on the night before you leave!

Suggested Items for Your Suitcase:

- Enough clothes for all the days of your trip, unless you will be doing laundry, plus any special clothes (dress up for the theatre, swimsuit, etc.)
- Underwear and socks for all the days, unless you will be doing laundry
- Sweater, fleece for layering
- Night clothes, robe, slippers if desired
- Tie or scarf, jewelry if needed, to "dress up"
- Extra shoes if needed: dress up, sandals, slippers, sports shoes
- Performance clothes, if necessary, in garment bag; don't forget socks and special shoes if needed
- Laundry bag
- 2 or 3 hangars

If necessary:

- Towel, wash cloth, soap
- Clothesline, laundry soap
- Swimsuit, cover-up, towel, hat, baseball cap, sun hat
- Sunscreen, sunblock, lip balm, after sun moisturizer, aloe vera gel

Optional but helpful:

- Sewing Kit, extra safety pins
- Small flashlight
- Grooming items: tweezers, nail clippers, manicure scissors, emery board, nail polish
- Extra feminine protection supplies
- Any other extra medication, first aid supplies, snacks

"Packing" Your Money belt

You will also need to "pack" your money belt. Items you will want to put in it:

- Ziplock bag to hold paper items
- Card with your name, address and phone number. Other "special" phone numbers need to be on the card too: parents' work numbers, other relatives numbers; bank and credit card account numbers and phone numbers to call if lost or stolen
- Medical insurance card and medical information: any diagnosis, medication and allergies
- Contact lens and/or eyeglass prescription
- Doctor's name and office phone number
- Passport or copy of information page of Passport
- Picture Identification Card
- Credit Card and back-up Credit Card
- ATM Card
- American Money
- Foreign Currency (sort by ziplock bag)

CHAPTER 10 - REMEMBER YOUR TRIP

WAYS TO REMEMBER YOUR TRIP

Photographs

One of the best ways to remember your trip is with photographs. However, there are a few things to remember that will make your photographs special and your photography experience more enjoyable.

The first thing to decide, especially for students, is if they really want to take a camera, and if so, what type. Some people are just not into taking pictures, but most will want to take at least some pictures. For adults the decision may be just how fancy they want to get with their camera and accessories, digital or not, and/or if they want to take a camcorder.

Camcorders can be really neat, but they are also heavy and take up quite a bit of room. Another problem is recharging the batteries. If you are determined to take yours be sure you have extra batteries and film, and a sturdy case to carry everything in. Be sure to keep track of it at all times! These are prime items for thieves. Don't forget a luggage tag!

For those who don't already have a camera, or who are not really into taking many pictures, the disposable cameras work really great. You can take two or three of these (be sure to write your name on each one) with you. They are relatively inexpensive, and take pretty good pictures.

However, if you think you will want to take a lot of pictures you will want to have a camera. Students may be able to borrow one from their parents, though parents need to consider if they will mind if that camera is lost or stolen. This may be a good time to get a camera as a gift.

There are so many different types of cameras on the market, with all kinds of features, so everyone really needs to consider their own needs and desires, and their own capabilities as a photographer.

A few features that are really nice to have are the red eye reduction feature, the option to turn the flash off, and the date feature. A built in telephoto lens is really nice too. A case to carry the camera and film in is very handy too, although a nice fanny pack can work very well, making it very easy to get to the camera and keeping your hands free. Whatever you use be sure to have your name and address inside the bag too, and a luggage tag on the outside.

The amount of film to take really depends upon the person but it is usually recommended to take one roll of film for each day of the trip. This may seem like a lot but when you are looking at a lot of sights you will be amazed at how many pictures you will want to take.

I suggest that you buy your film before you leave on your trip. You can usually find good sales on multipacks of film. It is very irritating to run out of film right in the middle of touring a sight, and sometimes it is hard to find film right away, or have time to buy it. Film is usually a lot cheaper here. Don't forget extra batteries! A standard lithium battery in a regular camera will usually last through about 15 rolls of film, though you need to consult the instructions for your own camera. If you are taking a lot of pictures, and using the telephoto and flash a lot, you may be surprised how quickly your battery runs out. Also, you may not know how many rolls of film your battery has already been used for when you start your trip.

Keeping track of fresh and exposed film is always a concern. The simplest way I have found, and that has worked wonderfully for my three sons too, is to use the "ziplock bag" method. You take two ziplock bags (quart size works best) and mark one with a permanent black marker "fresh" and the other one with a permanent red marker "exposed". Write your name on each bag too. Put all of your fresh film, in the film canisters, into the bag marked "fresh". Put an empty film canister into the "exposed" bag. Whenever you finish a roll of film you immediately put it into the empty canister in the "exposed" bag. Be sure to do this before you take out a fresh roll. It is very easy to mix up the film when you are in a hurry to change film. When you take out your fresh film you could put the empty canister in your camera bag or in the "exposed" bag, though it is hard to find the empty one when you have several in there.

You may also want to carry just one or two rolls of film in a quart sized ziplock bag with a sandwich sized ziplock bag inside that to hold exposed film for just that day. Mark "exposed" on the small bag in red. This can be carried in your daypack and all your other film and exposed film can be in your carry-on. At the end of each day move the exposed film into the other ziplock bag in your carry-on and restock the ziplock bag that goes in the daypack.

You want to figure out a method that will work well for you and will make it easy for you to change film quickly and safely, and to store your fresh and exposed film.

If you are concerned about putting your film through the x-ray machines at the airports there are special bags you can buy to put the film in. However, with all the concern about safety now, a clear ziplock bag works very well. You can simply hand it to the screener so it won't go through the machine and they can see what is in it very easily.

However you handle this just make sure all your film is together. A friend of mine became worried about having the film in her carry-on go through the x-ray machine. This would have been OK but she waited until we were in line and ready to go through the detector. She stopped in the line and began searching through her carry-on for all her film. Unfortunately her several rolls of film had fallen throughout her carry-on. People were very annoyed that she was holding up the line, and the person in charge of the scanner keep telling her that it was OK for the film to go through the x-ray machine. To make matters worse we were in British Columbia, Canada, and most everyone was speaking French, or heavily accented English. A frustrating way to start a flight.

I highly encourage everyone to practice with the camera they are going to use. Take a variety of pictures and have them developed to see how they turn out a while before you leave on your trip. Be sure to familiarize yourself with all the features of your camera so you can easily use it on the trip and you know that the camera is working properly. It is very disappointing to start taking pictures and find out that something is not working on your camera. Don't forget to take the instructions for your camera with you.

When you do take pictures try to take pictures of the sights you see with some of the members of your group in the pictures. When you look at them later you will probably enjoy the ones with your friends in them the most. Don't forget to take pictures of the housing sites you stay at, both indoors and outdoors.

You might want to take some pictures of the souvenirs that you buy just in case your luggage is lost on the return trip. This may help if you need to make a claim for lost items.

Sometimes at certain museums you may have to buy a "photography permit" that allows you to take pictures. If you want to take any pictures you will need to buy this permit. Don't push your luck and try to get away without buying one if you really intend on taking pictures. Your camera could be taken away by guards. Unfortunately, even after you buy the permit, you may get inside the museum and find out that you cannot take flash pictures of a lot of the displays, there may be some things you can.

You probably will not be allowed to take flash pictures at most of the museums, cathedrals, and theatres that you might visit. Sometimes there is a feature on your camera that allows you to take pictures without the flash. If you are going to try this make sure you are familiar with it. You can get in a lot of trouble if your flash accidentally goes off.

Be sure to budget in developing film when you get back. This can really be expensive when you have several rolls to develop. Do think a little about what you will do with all the pictures afterward. Sometimes people get doubles and then share with their friends. You will want to try to get your pictures organized and into an album, with some sort of labeling as soon as possible, because it is easy to forget what the sights are and who the people are in the pictures.

Journal

Writing down your experiences, thoughts and feelings about your trip can keep your memories alive, rather than disappearing into oblivion when your return home. You may think you will remember a lot of what happened on your trip but it can be quite a disappointment to realize how much you have forgotten even a few days after arriving home from the trip.

It is really helpful to take a few moments each day of the trip, maybe right before you go to bed, or during a long bus ride, to write down that day's experiences: what you saw, did, ate, observed, and how you felt about it. Try to write something each day, even if it is just a few lines, rather than getting behind and giving up because there is so much to catch up on. Having your itinerary in front of you is very helpful when you write.

Scrapbook

Scrapbook making has become a really popular thing to do with pictures and other memorabilia now. If you think that you may want to do this you will want to remember to save all your ticket stubs, brochures, patches, magnets, restaurant napkins, match books, stickers, price tags, receipts, shopping bags, postcards, to add to your scrapbook. Try carrying a manila envelope in your daypack to hold all this stuff.

CHAPTER 11 - CHAPERONE INFO

CHAPERONE SUGGESTIONS

Chaperones are a very important part of your trip with students. Well-prepared chaperones can be an immense asset for your trip but unfortunately unprepared ones can cause everyone a lot of grief.

Be sure to check with your School District if they require anyone chaperoning and/or accompanying students to have to fill out paperwork for a security clearance and/or be fingerprinted. They also may require any adults going on the trip to attend certain training meetings provided by the School District. If they do be sure to get the required forms as soon as possible and hand them out and ask for them back quickly. It may take awhile for the School District to process the forms. Set up any needed meetings so your adult travelers have ample time to follow all the procedures.

You need to try from the very beginning during the planning of the trip to make clear the expectations for the chaperones on the trip. Sometimes people just want to come on the trip because it sounds like a really neat experience. They may not really understand what is involved with chaperoning a group of students. It's up to you to let the adults know what will be expected of them before they sign up to chaperone so they will not be getting into something they really won't want to do.

Chaperone Responsibilities

Basically, chaperoning a group of students means watching out for the students assigned to you, as well as all the others, during the trip. You will need to check with the students assigned to you at night to make sure they are in their rooms at bed-check and pass on to them information about what is happening the next day. You'll also want to check on any health or injury problems and ask about other concerns too. Then you will want to make sure they are up in the morning and ready to go.

You might be asked to count the people on the buses when they have boarded after an event to make sure everyone is there, every time. You will be with them on all tours, meals, flights, though you may not be expected to stay with your assigned students all the time, just in the general vicinity.

You may have to stay in a room with students if the housing situation warrants it...usually rooms where there are more than four students. However, there should **always** be two adults together in situations like these. You probably won't have to stay with the students every minute while you are touring events but there may be times when you are asked to stay with a group of assigned students for certain situations.

When the group I was with traveled to England the students were given a lot of freedom to tour museums, castles, cathedrals, and even small towns without chaperones with them all of the time, although we were all in the general vicinity. However, when we were in London the students had to stay in assigned groups and with chaperones to visit different sites in the city.

You usually won't be expected to discipline the students, but if you encounter a situation where they are not behaving as they are expected you may need to talk to them and then possibly take them to the Leader of the group to discuss the situation. Most of the time you are not going to have any problems because the students really do want to have a good time and will be on their best behavior.

What may happen is they might get a little cranky from getting overly tired, hungry, being around too many people for too long. They may say things they shouldn't because they are still children and may not have the self-control that we would hope they would have. Some adults may act the same way too, unfortunately.

Dealing with Inappropriate Behavior

Sometimes all you need to say is "That's not appropriate behavior". If they don't stop, then say "That's not appropriate behavior and stop please." If they refuse to stop you may need to bring in the group Leader or another chaperone to discuss the situation. If the behavior does not improve, discussion and possible consequences will need to be dealt with by the Leader of the group.

Try to be considerate and patient but do stop inappropriate behavior right away. Don't wait until they've done it so many times you "can't take it anymore."

This is one reason why you want to have your trip as well planned as possible and your travelers prepared as much as possible. You want to try to make sure everyone will be able to get enough rest and to keep meals to a reasonable schedule. Sometimes things don't work out like you would like and you may need to change the schedule a little if needed to give everyone a chance to rest a little more if travelers are getting overly tired.

Sometimes you will just have to remind everyone that they need to really make an effort to be patient with each other and the situations they are in and to just enjoy the trip. Things will happen on the trip that may be irritating but everyone will need to "cope" with it and show how mature they can be.

If there are major violations of the Rules: smoking, drinking, taking illegal drugs, being in the opposite sex's room, then these will have to be dealt with by the Leader. Suggestions in how to deal with these situations are found in a later chapter called Rules and Guidelines.

Rules are generally basic school rules that are always in affect at school and at school sponsored activities. Violations of these rules can result in very severe consequences according to School District Policies. These Rules and the consequences of breaking them need to be reiterated again to the students and parents along with the possible consequences that will occur on the trip if these rules are broken.

The students should be given some written general Guidelines for Behavior also. These Guidelines are designed to help the students to know how they are to act in the various situations they will encounter while traveling. A description of these will be found in the chapter called Rules and Guidelines. It would be a good idea to discuss these Guidelines with the students and the chaperones together along with the parents.

Remind the students and the parents that in signing the Trip Contract they have agreed to follow these Rules and Guidelines and will accept the consequences if they do not follow them.

Sometimes during the trip they may need to be reminded that they did sign the agreement to follow the Rules and Guidelines for the trip. This reminder may be all they need to help improve their behavior.

Chaperone Behavior

Chaperone behavior is another matter. You would hope that you would not have any problems with the behavior of the chaperones on the trip. Most adults even considering going on a trip will realize that they too will need to be on their best behavior. After all, they will be asking the students to be on their best behavior too.

However, at the same time you may not know all the chaperones very well. Given that everyone may have slightly different expectations and understandings of what kind of behavior is expected it is sometimes helpful to write out some specifics.

Some groups have found it helpful for the chaperones to sign a Chaperone Agreement, similar to the one the students have been asked to sign in the Trip Contract. This form can cover the types of behaviors and responsibilities that will be expected of chaperones on the trip.

Chaperone Agreement

You may want to have your chaperones sign a form acknowledging they will agree to the kind of behaviors that are being asked of them. The following is a suggested form:

CHAPERONE ACKNOWLEDGMENT

I,_______________________________, understand that for the duration of

the____
(group field trip, location, date)
I am a chaperone and volunteer for the _____________(School District). I understand my duties include but are not limited to the following:

- Supervise students at all times, being sensitive to their medical state and budgetary needs
- Participate in training for chaperones provided by the District
- Enforce fairly the rules students must abide in accordance with School Board policy
- Refrain from the use of illegal drugs or alcohol for the duration of the trip
- Carry student emergency and health information with me at all times
- Deal with discipline and harassment in a fair and firm manner, and immediately, in accordance with School Board policy
- Not smoke in the presence of students
- Know the whereabouts of the students assigned to me at all times
- Communicate regularly with the director of the trip and the nurse regarding students assigned to me
- Act at all times in the best interest of the students, understanding that this is not a personal vacation
- Share necessary health information regarding myself with the nurse
- Follow the direction of the trip director and any designees

I understand that for the duration of this trip I will be operating as an agent of the__________(School District). As such, I will act within the scope of my duties as chaperone and supervisor of students and at the direction of the District.

_______________________________________ ____________________
Signature *Date*

Other Duties

If by chance chaperones will be asked to provide some of the security on the trip, such as "patrolling the halls" of the housing site after the bed-check time, you need to make this clear at the beginning of the trip. Some chaperones may not be willing to do this but they will need to understand that this is a necessary part of the trip and that all of the chaperones will be expected to do their share. This can be especially hard on everyone because "patrolling the halls" usually involves staying up a few hours after bed check. This means a shorter night's sleep and can be very tiring.

Potential chaperones need to be aware of these expected responsibilities before they sign up to go on the trip to chaperone, if possible. Sometimes situations will arise later during the planning of the trip but after chaperones have already committed to going on the trip. You need to keep the chaperones informed of situations that will directly affect them as much as possible. This will help in avoiding a lot of hard feelings and misunderstandings.

Chaperones are usually asked to carry copies of the Passports and medical forms of the students' assigned to them at all times. It is a good idea for each chaperone to have a partner that can carry a copy of their Passport and medical forms too. It is also very helpful to inform the partner of any medical conditions so at least one other person, beside the medical person, is aware of them. For example: asthma, diabetes, and allergies to bees or penicillin.

Chaperones usually look around at breakfast to see if their students are there, and if they don't see them they may want to go to their room to check to see if they are up.

At night it is really helpful for the Leader to meet with all the chaperones, instructors, etc. to pass on any additional information and to touch base with everyone. The next day's itinerary should be discussed, along with wake up times and times to be on the buses ready to go. Any problems need to be discussed and specific concerns discussed privately with the leader.

This meeting needs to be kept as short as possible since the students will be unaccompanied at this time.

At bed check time chaperones should talk to their assigned students about any concerns they might have: health, money problems, etc. and review with them the next day's itinerary and what is expected of them. Be sure to remind them of the wake-up time and what time they need to be on the bus.

Alcohol Questions

An area you must discuss with your chaperones as well as any other adults going on the trip, instructors included, is the situation of adults drinking alcoholic beverages at any time on the trip. This can be a very sticky situation because people can have very different views on the subject and can get very emotional about it.

Many times a trip overseas is viewed as a cultural experience and that travelers should experience the cultures of the various countries they are visiting. Sometimes in foreign countries drinking wine or beer is an accepted part of the culture and just about everyone has a drink with their meal. Sometimes even students, especially if they are traveling with a group made up of their foreign language class, may need to consider this issue because it would be a part of the culture they are studying. This is especially true if students will be having Home stays with local families. In these situations it is particularly important to discuss drinking with the parents. Some groups I know of have had parents sign a permission form if they will allow their students to drink alcoholic beverages in a foreign country.

Otherwise the issue of students drinking on a trip is simply a violation of school rules and is not allowed. Sometimes students have a hard time understanding this if they are over age eighteen. In most foreign countries and on international flights the drinking age is eighteen. However, students need to understand that if this is a school sponsored trip they are still subject to school rules and should not drink even if they are of a legal age to drink.

For adults however, they are of legal age and it just becomes a matter of whether this is something that should be allowed when they are a part of a student trip. The problem with drinking is that you never know how someone is going to react when they have had a drink or two. There may be no problems but you just never know.

The students well being and safety should be the first and foremost responsibility of all the adults going on the trip. Having all adults going on the trip abstain from drinking alcoholic beverages for the entire trip, including the flights, may be the best solution all around.

One question that always comes up is "what about the times when a chaperone or instructor is "off duty"? This could be considered to be the time when there is a hired security group "watching" the rooms of the students. Some may want to visit a local Pub during these "off hours".

While this may seem to be an OK idea it can come back to cause you a lot of problems. First of all you cannot control the amount of drinks a person may have or the reactions they may have to even just one. Their reactions may carry over to the events on the next day.

Secondly, adults are really never "off duty" when it comes to being responsible for the students on the trip. Sure enough when the adults decide to visit a Pub that will be the night when some of the students need them in the middle of the night. You just never know what is going to happen with students.

Here is an example of what happened on one trip with a group of 8th graders visiting Washington DC. The group had hired security guards to watch to make sure no students left their rooms after 11:00 PM. The adults on the trip decided to visit the Karaoke Bar located at the top of the hotel.

In the meantime one of the security guards (who happened to be a "fill in" for that night) agreed to let a few of the students go into each others' rooms, boys and girls, while the chaperones were upstairs, if they would pay him a certain amount of cash. The students confessed the next day. The guard was fired and the students had to miss one of the tours and stay with the Leader and one of the chaperones the whole day. The parents were also called and informed of the situation.

It probably wouldn't have happened if the adults had been in their rooms because they would have heard what was going on. Also, some of the students knew that the adults were going up to the bar so they felt that they might be able to "get away with it."

Chaperone Chain of Command

If you have several chaperones going on the trip you will want some sort of "chain of command" to facilitate communication throughout the group. Usually a good ratio would be to have six to eight adults report to one adult. You could have a "head" chaperone, with maybe one or two "assistants", depending upon the total number of chaperones. The same would go for instructors and any other adults that might be going on the trip. These adults would then report to the Leader and convey any information as needed.

Usually this would be needed in the mornings to let the Leader know that everyone is up, accounted for, and ready to go for the day. Chaperones would have their assigned students' check in with them in the morning when they are ready to board the buses. Chaperones would then report to the adult that they are assigned to report to and tell them their group is ready to go. Those adults then report to the Leader. The chain of command could be used at any other time during the trip as needed.

Bits and Pieces

Chaperones need to board the bus before the students, and especially the first time, to choose their seats. I've found that it usually works best to have chaperones sit in the front seat and in another seat about half way back. If you have more than four chaperones per bus then you might have them sit one third and two thirds back in the bus, as well as in the front seat. Chaperones should sit together, not with students, if possible. It is a lot more fun for chaperones to have a partner to sit with. Students really don't like sitting with adults. If you have extra seats a chaperone may want to sit alone.

Chaperones can get on and put their bags, coats, to mark their seats and then get off and let the students get on and choose their seats. It is not really a good idea to save seats for students, even your own children. This is a good way to get a lot of students mad at you before the trip even gets started. I have seen this happen and there were a lot of hurt feelings among students and chaperones.

Every time the bus stops and anyone gets off, the chaperones need to make sure they have taken a count of all those on the bus, students, chaperones, any other adults. This number should always be the same unless you have allowed someone to change buses. Report to the Leader as he/she comes to each bus if everyone is there and especially if the count isn't correct. Usually you will know who is missing.

If at any time a bus leaves a site and some of the people stay back for some reason be sure to take a count before the bus leaves, or at least before people start getting off at the next stop. Then you will know how many need to get back on the bus when you leave there. This is very important! When I was on the England trip we arrived early at our housing site at a youth hostel. The dinner we were to have was not ready yet so the Leader had the buses take the students into the town to look around. It was a really neat historical town but when we got there most of the shops were closed. Unfortunately some of the adults had stayed back at the housing site, which we chaperones didn't realize until people had gotten off the bus at the town. We didn't have any idea how many had come with us. We were just lucky that everyone came back on time to board the buses to go back to the hostel and we weren't missing anyone when we returned.

Be particularly aware if people are getting on and off the bus. Sometimes you might think everyone is there but someone may have slipped off the bus for some reason. Don't count until you are sure everyone should be there. Have everyone sit down in their seats and don't let anyone get off at that point. If they absolutely need to get off you will need to do a new count when they come back. I know of instances where students were left because they had been on the bus then realized they had left their sunglasses on a bench so they got off the bus. The chaperones didn't think they were gone, and when students said some were missing they mistakenly said that they probably got on another bus. This is why you need to have assigned buses!!!

One thing that I have found important to remember as a chaperone is to try to remain as calm and relaxed as possible, even when there are problems. Students are very sensitive to your moods and if they sense that you are upset then they may become upset too. If there is a situation of concern you need to make every effort to stay as calm as possible. Evaluate the situation and discuss with other chaperones and the Leader what needs to be done.

Chaperones have found it very helpful to carry a few extra plastic shopping bags and quart size ziplock bags with them. The shopping bags can be used to put extra garbage in from the buses (have the students pick it up, or pass the bags up and down the aisles.) They are very handy if someone gets sick too. Ziplock bags are handy for holding things and can also be used for students to pass around the bus to collect a tip for the bus driver. Extra tissues are nice to have too, as well as a couple extra pens.

Advice for Chaperones Who Are Parents of Students on the Trip

Sharing in the experiences of a group trip with your own children who are also students can be a wonderful, memorable and enjoyable time for all of you. However, expectations need to be discussed between parents and students so the trip doesn't turn into a frustrating, hurtful and disappointing experience.

Many times students may be fearful that their parents will be "hovering" around them all the time, telling them what to do, and possibly embarrassing them in front of their friends. With good communication and respectful behavior among everyone this does not have to be the case.

Most of the time the chaperones will be with other chaperones, enjoying the sights with the large group. Generally students will not have to stay in their assigned chaperone groups while touring, except in specific situations when the large group breaks down into smaller groups to tour different things.

Also, parents should discuss with their own students if they want their parent to be their assigned chaperone. A parent may want their student to get to know another chaperone and vice versa. Their student may also be of the opposite sex and will have a chaperone assigned to them of the same sex.

Students may want to spend most of their time with their friends. However, they may also want to spend certain times with their parents. Parents need to be sensitive to their children's feelings and act accordingly. One suggestion would be for a parent to simply just check in with their child at the end of the day to see how things are going. Once the student realizes that the parent isn't going to "hover" over them they may be more willing to talk and even spend more time with their parent on the trip.

One thing I would recommend that you avoid doing is keeping all the money and making your student come to you every day for their "daily allotment". I have seen parent chaperones do this to their children and the students were very embarrassed about it. All their friends had to handle their own money and budget it out over the trip. These students wanted to be treated like all the other students. It really was a "control issue" among some of the parents. They felt that this made their student have to come to them and talk to them. Please think about this if you are considering doing this, even if you feel your student can be really irresponsible with money. They may surprise you with how well they will do given the chance.

I gave my boys a certain amount of money at the beginning of a trip to cover meals, snacks and a small amount for souvenirs. They usually brought more of their own money to spend on additional souvenirs. We talked about how they should budget it out to have enough for all the meals for which they had to pay. (The trips we went on usually did not have all the meals provided, so there were many we had to budget for.)

They also understood that if there was something really special that they found that they wanted they could come to me to see if I would put it on a credit card. Sometimes I did! Also, towards the end of the trip I discussed with them how their budgeting was going and if they needed more money. Sometimes they had more left than I did. Occasionally I might need to give them a little more if we had had unanticipated expenses.

In London my son Jon found a leather jacket that he really wanted at the Hard Rock Café. We had told him that we would buy him a leather jacket sometime, though I hadn't thought we'd find one on the trip. Since it was a little more than I had planned on spending we agreed that he would pay for half of it when we got back home. That jacket has remained one of his most valued possessions.

CHAPTER 12 - LOGISTICS

GROUP LOGISTICS

Traveling with any large group requires a little more logistical planning than with a small group or family. However with some advance preparation things can go pretty smoothly. Areas you need to consider are tour bus assignments, room assignments and assigned jobs for everyone on the trip, which helps to spread out the workload.

Getting to the Airport

You will need to decide if you want the parents to take their student to the airport at the beginning of the trip, or if you want to provide bus transportation for everyone. Unless the airport is really close, and your group is not very large, you will want to arrange for bus transportation for everyone. That way you will know that everyone will arrive at the airport at the right time and in the right place.

You will also want to decide if you want parents to pick up their students at the airport at the end of the trip, or if you need to provide bus transportation back to the school. This may be more of an issue now with increased airport security. At this time no one can go to the arrival or departure gates to greet travelers. You can only meet them at the baggage pick-up area. Airports are also extremely busy places and expensive places to park if you have to wait for very long.

You will probably want to have everyone meet at the school or another place that has a large parking lot. You will need space for everyone, and all their luggage, before they board the bus, or buses. Be sure to allow enough time for meeting, traveling to the airport and checking in!!!

If you are able to get everyone in your group on the same flight this part will go very smoothly. However, usually a large group will not be put on the same flight, so you will need to plan accordingly. If the flights are taking off within a few hours of each other then you may still be able to have everyone leave for the airport at the same time. If not, you may need to arrange for bus pick-ups of the separate groups at different times. There will need to be someone "in charge" of each group, with chaperones checking in to him or her.

If there is more than one flight the Leader may need to leave on the first flight out so he/she can arrive and check on the housing. Other chaperones will need to be in charge of the other flight(s).

When the group arrives at the airport everyone will need to check in. With increased security at airports now everyone's checked bag may also be searched. Remind everyone to be prepared for this and to have his or her luggage keys handy. The airline may have arranged for a special check in area for the group, or you may have to join the line of other travelers checking in and checking their bags. At check in everyone will have to show Picture Identification and their Passport if you are leaving the country. Everyone will probably be asked questions about packing their own suitcases. Remind them that they did pack their own bag, even if their mom helped them. Remind the group to stay together until they have checked in and then they need to head for the departure gate and the metal detector security check point.

The same kind of brightly colored yarn tied to each suitcase can come in very handy to indicate which bags belong to your group, especially if you are waiting in a long line. Students are notorious for setting their luggage down and wandering off. The colored yarn is also very helpful during baggage retrieval at baggage claim at the airport too.

At this point everyone will be going through the security checkpoint and metal detectors. Remind the students to not say anything stupid and to be patient and cooperate with the utmost courtesy.

Once at the departure gate you may have quite a bit of time before you leave. Try to keep everyone together in a group, with all their carry-ons. This way if some of them need to use the restroom or get something to eat others will be there to watch their stuff. Give everyone a time when they all need to be back at the gate for departure.

Airplane Seating

The Leader will need to decide how to handle the seating on the airplane. The airline may give you the tickets with assigned seats in a number of configurations. Sometimes they are alphabetical, with adults along with the students, sometimes separate. They may be in blocks of seats, or they may be in groups of seats: fives, fours, threes, and twos.

The first decision you will need to make is if you will allow everyone to change from his or her assigned seats. I have been on trips where everyone sat in their assigned seats and on trips where everyone could trade around before they got on the plane.

I would personally recommend that you allow everyone to choose who they want to sit by. This will add a little extra work for you or someone you designate, but in the end everyone will be a lot happier, including the chaperones.

You will need to discuss this with the Travel Agent and/or the airline before you get there to find out if they will allow your travelers to board with someone else's boarding pass, and to sit in a different seat than they have been assigned. If the airline will not then you will have no choice in the matter. Some Travel Agents may ask for seating choices ahead of time and have the boarding passes ready when you check in.

If they can board with another's boarding pass then the simplest way to handle this is to go through the tickets and if they are arranged in groups organize them by the groups of twos, threes, etc. Ask your chaperones and students to organize themselves in the groups they wish to sit in (by twos, threes, etc.) and then come to you for those boarding passes in those groups. They can work out the seating arrangements in their group.

If the boarding passes are arranged in blocks of seats you may want to hand out the passes and have everyone arrange among themselves where, and by whom, they wish to sit.

If everyone has to have their own boarding pass you may want to allow them to change seats after they have boarded. This could cause quite a problem with the other passengers because everyone is trying to put their luggage in the overhead bins and get to their seats, so you may want to avoid this if possible. Some groups have allowed people to change seats after the plane is in the air and the seatbelt sign off. This may, or may not cause a lot of problems. Make sure everyone knows they need to ask the person they want to trade with if it is OK and if it is not then "don't push it". Remind them that they are not to ask anyone who is not from the group to trade seats!

Stress to everyone in your group that they are not the only ones on the plane and they need to be very respectful of all the other passengers and flight attendants. Remind them that flight attendants are not their personal servants, they don't need to continually "call" them to get them something.

After landing remind everyone to stay together in the group until you all get to the baggage claim area. When you have arrived at that area you will need chaperones to check to see if all their assigned students are there. Have everyone stay in a designated area while those students assigned with the job of retrieving luggage off the carousel take their positions.

Have two to four students grab the group's luggage as it comes off the carousel. This is where the brightly colored yarn comes in. The student helpers will know which luggage to grab, and won't make the other passengers angry by taking off the wrong luggage. Once they have grabbed the luggage other students can move the bags back out of the way and over to the group. You might want a "chain" of six to eight to slide the luggage to the group.

Once the luggage is with the group everyone can start claiming their own bags. It might be helpful to have them stand in another spot, with their luggage, so you will know who hasn't gotten their luggage yet.

If your transportation to your housing site is there you may want to instruct those who have their luggage to begin getting on the buses. It would be a good idea for students to check in with their chaperone after getting their luggage and are ready to board the buses.

You may want certain students loading the buses as part of their "jobs". Remind everyone to get his or her bags as close to the buses as possible. There are still lots of other people around this area and you don't want the bags in everyone else's way, or left out for a thief to take. This will work only if the "loaders" have their bags to begin with and can proceed to the buses, choose their seats, leave their carry-ons at their seat and begin loading the other luggage. If not, others may have to help out.

Hopefully everyone's luggage will have arrived and you all can proceed to the housing site. If there are any missing items the Leader will need to contact airport personnel for the procedures to follow.

If you have any instruments, shipping crates and boxes that are also arriving, you will need to have someone check on these too, and check on the transportation that you have arranged for all these items. You should have assigned "instrument loaders". They will need to get their own luggage on the buses first then proceed to help with the instruments, etc. Then all the instruments and shipping crates will need to be taken to the transportation you have arranged. Hopefully it will be parked nearby.

Tour Buses

I have found that it is very helpful to have assigned buses for all travelers before the trip begins. You will need to find out the maximum number the tour buses you are using will seat. Sometimes you may have buses that will seat different numbers of people too, within your group. Be sure to get an accurate number for each bus from your Travel Agent.

Have sign-up sheets posted at your group meetings. Ask the chaperones and instructors to sign up first, before the students. After all the chaperones and instructors have signed up, and arranged themselves out evenly throughout the buses, the students may then sign up. Remind everybody that they will need to stay on their assigned bus throughout the trip unless they receive special permission to change from the chaperones on each bus. You may want to have them sign up with their assigned chaperone groups on the same bus as their chaperone.

Sometimes situations come up where travelers may need to change buses. If there is room on another bus there is no reason why this should not be allowed. But you want to encourage everyone to try to stay with his or her assigned bus. This is simply because it makes it much easier to keep track of everyone when they are getting on and off the buses. Usually very few will want to change buses, especially if they have been given the opportunity to choose a bus from the beginning.

The transportation from the airport to the first housing site, and then back to the airport at the end of the trip may be a different configuration than the tour buses for the main part of the trip. Ask the Travel Agent if he or she knows of any changes in the buses, especially if they will hold different amounts of people. Also, if you will be arriving on different flights at different times, the bus assignments may be different too. You may just have to have everyone get onto the buses as quickly as possible without bothering with bus assignments. You will need to be especially careful at this time to make sure you have everyone on the buses before you leave. It will be especially important to know the exact number of travelers you have getting on the buses. When you count those on each bus the numbers should add up correctly. If they don't, you will have to take more counts and try to determine who is missing.

It is helpful to have at least two chaperones count everyone when they get back on the buses and sit down. Usually one can count from the back and the other count from the front, walking down the aisle. Hopefully they will come up with the right number for that bus. This count must be taken **every** time travelers get off the bus and then get back on.

It is very important that chaperones do remember to count every time, after everyone has returned to the bus. It is recommended not to start counting too soon, before everyone is seated, because it is very easy to get mixed up. Also, listen to those on the bus if they say someone is missing. Usually someone will notice, though not always. I know of instances where students were left behind because chaperones either didn't count carefully, or they didn't listen to the students when they said that someone was missing.

People really are creatures of habit and you will see this on the buses. Invariably everyone will sit in the same seats that they start out with, with a minimum amount of changing. This can be very helpful for the chaperones to determine who is missing when they are taking a count on a bus. However there is usually no need to have assigned seats.

Sometimes a bus may have an unusual seating arrangement. There may be tables on the bus, or "special" front seats. In England one of the buses was a "double-decker" type with a smaller seating compartment below with two tables up above and special seats up front. For this bus we asked students and chaperones to move around a little to allow those that wanted to have a turn at the table seats and the front seats. This worked fine for those that wanted to move around, though some did not care if they sat in those seats or not.

It would be helpful to go over the basic manners of consideration when riding on airplanes and buses with all the travelers. These would include picking up any garbage, not continually getting into the overhead storage bins, talking softly, considering those around them when they turn the individual overhead lights on, not tilting the seats back very far (this is very uncomfortable for those sitting behind them), not pressing their knees against the seat in front of them and maybe other suggestions.

Something that may be helpful if you have two or more buses is to give each person pieces of brightly colored yarn to tie to all the pieces of their luggage: suitcase, carry-on, daypack. These can be color coded for each of the buses. This will help in getting the correct luggage on the right bus. This same colored yarn can also help in retrieving luggage off the luggage carousel at the airport if you fly.

Room Assignments

You may or may not be able to submit a room assignment list ahead of time to your housing sites. Sometimes a hotel will have you submit one and have all the room numbers assigned when you get there. Other times when you arrive they will give you a set of numbers and you will have to make assignments then. A housing site such as a youth hostel may give you the different configurations (rooms of 4, 6, 8, ?) available to you before you leave on the trip. You will be able to make these assignments before you leave and then match them up with the room numbers. In any case you will need to be flexible and organized in this area. Sometimes room number assignments may change when you get there.

It will be very helpful for the Leader to take with them several copies of the chosen roommate assignments from the students and the chaperones. Each chaperone needs a few copies of these too. At each housing site chaperones will want to write down the room numbers of the students and other chaperones, and especially the nurse and the Leader.

When you arrive at a housing site you will check-in and find out how they have arranged the room assignments. If you are just given a list of numbers you might want to look over the rooms first to see the layout and then make room assignments. If at all possible try to put males and females on separate floors. Mix chaperones' rooms throughout. Hopefully all of your rooms will be close by and not spread throughout a large complex.

Once you have decided upon room assignments you will want to meet with the entire group and read off the room numbers and then have each set of roommates come up and check with you or your designee and receive their keys. It may be simpler to have them stay on the bus and then give out the room numbers and keys as they leave the buses. If the housing site has made the room assignments already they may want each set of roommates to check in with them and receive their keys.

Chaperones should be writing down the room numbers for their assigned group as well as any other room numbers that they want to know. They should also write down the room numbers for the other chaperones and especially the nurse/medical person and trip Leader.

If it is possible, arrange for "wake up" calls to every room for the next morning. Usually 90 minutes before the scheduled time to leave is sufficient. Travelers can always get up earlier if they need to. If calls are unavailable arrange for a chaperone or two to knock on each door the next morning. They need to wait until they hear a response from inside the room before they go on to the next room. Be sure they have a list of the correct room numbers assigned to your group!!!

You will need to check with the housing site as to the procedure for check out and pass this on to the travelers. If you are checking out the next morning you will need to explain the procedures to everyone when you have your large group meeting. If you are going to be at the housing site a few nights then you will be able to let everyone know the procedures for check out at your next group meeting. You can also pass the information on to the chaperones to inform the students at the bed-check time the night before you leave that particular housing site. Don't forget a reminder about leaving a tip if tips are expected.

If there is any concern that students may leave a big mess in their hotel room, or damage anything, you may need chaperones to check their assigned students' rooms before they check out in the morning. A reminder the night before to clean up their garbage before they check out may be all that's needed.

Home stays will require a little more organization. If you have given a list of your travelers to the Home stay Coordinator they may have already made assignments. You will want to make sure that the Leader has a copy of the assignments with them at all times. Students need to know that if they have any problems with the Home stay assignment they need to discuss it with their chaperone and/or the Leader as soon as possible. Hopefully everything will go smoothly with everyone involved. Remind the students that this is a learning experience and they need to be as flexible as possible. Before you leave on the trip remind everyone to take thank you cards and maybe small gifts for their host families.

Housing Security

Sometime after the check in time the Leader and maybe a few chaperones will need to take a look at the security issue at the housing site. The safety of everyone is the paramount concern. Consider not just the idea of students trying to get into each other's rooms after bed-check time, but also the issue of other guests at the housing site bothering the students.

If you have already arranged for security guards to go on duty after bed-check time then you don't have too much to worry about. If not then you need to look over the housing site and determine how many adults you will need to "patrol" the halls until you are reasonably sure all the students are asleep.

One suggestion is that after bed-check time you may want someone to place strips of tape on each door of students' rooms at the top and towards the bottom. You can usually tell if someone came out the door before they were supposed to. This may be enough to deter them.

If all your assigned rooms are on a few floors this will make security a lot easier. One of the worst security situations I have heard of was a group in a hotel with rooms that all opened to outside walkways and the student's rooms were spread throughout the large hotel. Several chaperones had to station themselves outside, spread out over the grounds of the hotel, to watch the doors for a few hours after bed-check.

You will want to set up some kind of a schedule for chaperones to be on "guard duty" so that each person will only have to do it a few times during the trip.

Be sure to let the students know that there will be adults patrolling the halls and remind them that they are not to let anyone else in their rooms.

Meals

Meals are a big deal with a large group. If everyone is eating at the same place it needs to be large enough to seat everyone together, or you will need to have 2 or 3 sittings, scheduled at different times to accommodate everyone. Usually the extra sittings would be at hotels or youth hostels if your group is very large and there is not enough room for your group and any other guests in their dining rooms at the same time.

Provided meals are usually buffet style, but not always. Breakfasts are usually buffet style, with a certain length of time given to your group, though there may be others there. Dinners may be buffet style or sit down, with certain choices of entrees given to everyone. Meals could also be cafeteria style, where guests choose what they want from the choices available and each item has a separate price. This might occur when the Travel Agent is there to pay for the bill when everyone is done eating.

Sometimes travelers will be on their own for a meal, usually lunch. Hopefully the Travel Agent will have checked to see that there are enough restaurants and cafes within the area for the entire group to have the meal within the prescribed time limit. While there may be familiar fast food style restaurants nearby it is always nice to try local eating places for a taste of that country's cuisine.

It is important to allow enough time in the scheduled itinerary for the meal breaks. It takes quite a bit of time for a large group to have a meal. If at all possible let the eating places nearby know the approximate time your group will be arriving and how many are in your group. This probably will not be possible when everyone is on their own, but if it is a scheduled stop be sure they know ahead of time.

Snacks and beverages can be purchased at local grocery stores, drug stores, bakeries, roadside stands (encourage everyone to be careful here…proper sanitation), gift shops, housing gift shops, and vending machines.

Sightseeing

Sightseeing is great fun and may take many different avenues with a large group. You may tour something as a large group, or you may break into smaller groups for private tours. You may want everyone to stay together with the large group or be in smaller groups moving at their own pace through a landmark or sight. Other times you may simply allow everyone to divide into even smaller groups and tour a small town.

Whatever the situation everyone needs to discuss beforehand safety instructions so everyone knows what to do if they become separated from the group, or cannot find their way back to the pick up site.

The most important thing that everyone needs to know, and follow, is to **always** be with at least one other person **at all times.** This is a rule that must be followed, no exceptions!

Everyone should have the itinerary with them at all times too, so they will know where they are supposed to be at the next stop, or the housing site. If they are separated from the group and cannot find the pick up spot, at least they will know where they will need to be. The phone number of the housing site should be on the itinerary so they can call there if they need to.

When leaving the buses be sure everyone knows the time that everyone is expected to be back and exactly where the buses will be parked. Encourage everyone to write down the address or at least the street names so if they can't figure out how to find their way back they can ask a local for directions.

There should be some sort of suggestions as to procedures to follow if anyone does become lost. Everyone should at least try to return to the pick up spot, even if they know they will be late. The buses will probably wait as long as they possibly can. A few members of the group may need to stay at the pick up site to wait for the missing members, with the understanding that someone will return for them. They will need to take a taxi to the housing site after a certain amount of time has passed.

Members may be instructed to call the housing site and explain what has happened and wait for instructions, or take a taxi themselves to the housing site.

Local authorities may need to be notified if the missing members have not been heard from after a certain length of time.

If the group is in a country with a different language remind everyone to have their "foreign language translation book" with them at all times.

Performances, Competitions, Tournaments, Exhibitions

If your group will be performing or competing extra time must be allowed for set up and take down, changing into and out of performance clothes, costumes, uniforms, as well as the actual event. Hopefully your Travel Agent and/or the Event Coordinator of your particular group will have arranged all the venues. Be aware that sometimes things don't run as smoothly as we would like especially when we are dealing with different languages and cultures. Just encourage everyone to do his or her best and enjoy the experience.

Trip Jobs

It is very helpful to have jobs assigned to everyone on the trip. Chaperones and instructors will need to know who to report to for any questions too. Spreading out the various jobs will help everyone to feel a part of the trip and will help everything to go smoothly.

Jobs to consider would be:

- Four to eight students to load the luggage into the luggage bays on the buses
- Four to eight students to unload the luggage at the housing sites
- Six to eight students to pull luggage off the airport carousel and pass them down to a designated spot (this helps keep all your travelers away from the luggage carousel when there are lots of other passengers waiting for their luggage too; each bag will need some sort of identifying mark, brightly colored yarn works well)
- Two + students per bus to pick up any garbage left on the bus each night
- Four to eight students to help with the loading and unloading of any instruments
- A few students to take care of any extra instruments, uniform cases, supplies that will need to be set up and taken down for any performances
- A few students to help prepare and pack any instruments, uniforms and supplies for the trip

Hopefully you will be able to find jobs for **all** the students going on the trip. If you don't you might have different students do some of the above jobs on different days. You just don't want it to be too confusing as to who is doing which job which day.

Helpful Information

It will be very helpful for everyone to carry an itinerary of the trip with them at all times. Not only does this keep them informed as to what is happening next on the trip, there should be phone numbers of the tour company and housing sites printed on it. This may not be practical all of the time so it may be helpful to print up small cards with trip phone numbers on it to be carried in the money belt. If your Travel Agency has a phone number you can contact them with on the trip have this number on the card too. You might want to have a brief calendar with the housing sites on it and the phone numbers of each. If you know you will have cellular phone service and someone on the trip is carrying one you may want to put this number on it too. The phone number of a school administrator "back home" may be helpful too.

You probably will be able to get cellular phone service just about anywhere in the United States, but you may not in foreign countries. Be sure to check with your Travel Agency and your cellular phone company.

These phone numbers are very important should anyone in your group become separated from the group and need to get in contact. It would be very frightening to be lost in a large city and not know who to call or even where the group is staying. Chances are you may not be able to remember the housing site name either.

Chaperone Paperwork

To help the trip go smoothly for everyone it will be helpful for the chaperones to carry a certain amount of papers. They need to know about this ahead of time so they will have room for a folder of papers.

Each person should have some sort of sturdy folder to hold the papers. They won't need to carry all of the papers all of the time, but to have them handy in their carry-on. They should carry copies of Passport pages and medical histories of their assigned students with them at all times, however.

Papers they will need to carry in the folder:

- Extra itinerary
- Alphabetical list of everyone on the trip, including chaperones
- Alphabetical list of those assigned to their bus
- List of everyone with their assigned roommates: so they can write the room numbers of the rooms at the housing site next to the groups. If there is more than one housing site you may want to have extra lists

Don't forget to carry an extra pen or pencil and a pad of paper to write information down. If you have questions, ask, **don't assume anything!!**

Communicating Home

Students and adults may want to call home at least once. This can be very expensive, depending upon where you are. Calling cards usually work great, provided they will work in that particular country. Sometimes Tour Groups will provide a calling card for each traveler. Remind everyone to check to make sure theirs will work where they are going. Calling cards, called PIN phone cards, may be purchased in different countries when you get there too, and usually offer good rates.

When calling from a foreign country you can usually ask for an English speaking operator. The directions should be printed by the phone. Travel guidebooks will usually have good directions on how to use the phone also. If you do not have cellular phone service you might find it cheaper to buy an inexpensive phone with a limited number of minutes available in the country(s) you will be visiting.

Be sure to remind everyone about the time difference from the country you may be calling from to back home. They may forget that their family may not be home, or may be sound asleep when they want to call.

On one trip I heard about, somebody took a laptop computer along and intended to send daily updates home for the group's parents to be able to access via email. Unfortunately it was sometimes difficult to find access to the Internet when he had the time to do it, so the updates weren't always available. Some of the parents got upset when they weren't able to get email about the trip every day.

If you are going to attempt sending information home like this be sure to make it clear that it may not work out to have daily updates. Also, be clear in whatever information that you send home. Parents can "read" a lot into what is written and may worry needlessly.

INDIVIDUAL LOGISTICS

Traveling with a group is a little different than traveling by yourself or with a small group of family and/or friends. Having yourself as prepared as possible before you leave on the trip, as well as keeping yourself as organized on the trip as possible will go a long ways in helping you to have a very enjoyable trip. One of the main things you will want to do on a large group trip is to make sure that you are **never** the one to make the whole group late for anything. Make sure that you are always early to get on the bus and early to every activity, with all the things you will need.

Other important things to remember are to study your itinerary very carefully so you know what is going on each day, and to listen carefully to all instructions and information given by the group leader, chaperones, instructors, tour guides and bus drivers.

Lots of times your attitude will be what determines how much you enjoy the trip. Some things may be irritating and not quite what you expected, but if you determine that you are going to make the most of it and enjoy everything as much as possible you will have a good time. Your personal self-discipline and maturity will be very evident here. Try your best, you **can** handle these experiences and have fun.

The following are some suggestions that you may find helpful in traveling with a large group, or in other situations also.

Luggage

Make sure you can manage all of your luggage by yourself. Even if your parent(s) are on the trip as chaperones don't expect them to carry any of your bags. Your luggage is your responsibility and you need to be able to handle it all by yourself. You will need to be able to carry everything, or at least roll it all together when you are going from place to place. This is very important in a large group because you will be moving as a group so you can't be making extra trips back to the luggage carousel or housing site, for instance, when you are getting ready to load the bus.

Airplane

Enjoy where you are seated, no matter who you are by, or what seat you are in. Everyone can't always have a window. If you are not thrilled with you seatmates then read, listen to your CD's, or maybe sleep. The flight will be over soon.

Remember to get all of your stuff together when it is time to leave the plane, your mom will not be checking behind you to see if you left anything. Watch out for things that slip down between seats.

Tour Buses

Hopefully you will like your seat partner(s) and enjoy talking with them. Be mindful of those around you. Don't talk too loud, tilt your seat back, or leave your overhead light on when everyone else's is off.

Be early when you need to board the buses and take your seat and stay there. Don't leave the bus unless told to. Let the chaperones know who might be missing. Be nice to the chaperones, they have a tough job, though it may not seem so to you. Remember any belongings you might put in the overhead bins or under the seat. Pick up your garbage and put it in the trash bin on the bus or take it off and dispose of it properly.

Housing

Don't spread your belongings all over the room. You probably will be pretty crowded if you are in a room for four so find yourself a spot for your stuff and try to keep everything altogether.

Here are some additional hints to make your stay more enjoyable:

- Check the way out in case of a fire; there should be a map on the inside of the door.
- Decide who will be in charge of the key(s). You will usually be given only one or two keys.
- Put your garbage in the provided containers, or in sacks next to it. Don't leave it all over the room.
- Ask for extra towels if you need them by calling the number provided.
- Put away any valuables and money when you leave the room for the day. Lock your suitcase if you want.
- Work out a shower schedule with your roommates. You probably don't want to have all of you taking a shower in the morning…someone will have to get up really early.
- Be in your room before bed-check time.
- Share with your roommates in leaving an appropriate tip.
- If you have free time to spend in the common areas of your housing be courteous to all you encounter.
- Don't stay up late talking or watching movies, try to go to sleep soon after bed-check time; you'll be glad you did the next morning

I have found that the key to a good travel day is found in proper preparation the night before. No matter how tired you are that night you still need to get everything ready for the next morning **before** you go to bed. (You will be a lot more tired, and not really thinking as clearly in the morning.) To do this: check over the next day's itinerary so you know what you will need. Get out the clothes you plan on wearing. Check over your performance clothes if you need them. Check over your budget and get out the money you will need from your money belt. Look over your daypack and add any additional items you might need: extra clothes, film, snacks and water.

If you will be leaving that housing site the next morning get all your stuff packed up except for what you will need the next morning. This will save you a lot of hassle, and maybe give you a little extra sleep time. Get up early enough so you don't want to have to rush to get to breakfast and/or the bus.

Sightseeing

Be sure to stay with at least one other person **at all times** and with a small group if possible, for safety. Allow yourself enough time to see what you want to see, as well as time to visit the gift shop if you desire. Keep track of the time!!!

Try to find out what is really important to see at the different places you will be visiting and make a point of seeing them first. If possible, write down what you saw in your journal and your feelings about it, as soon as you can. Take pictures if you want but be sure to keep track of your camera and daypack all the time.

Meals

It is most likely on this trip that you will be responsible for yourself for your meals. This means that your mom, even if she is on the trip, is not going to be asking you if you have gotten enough to eat, or are eating the right stuff. You will be given opportunities to eat and sometimes additional choices as to where you will get to eat. Traveling with a group of your friends can sometimes help, and unfortunately, sometimes hinder you in eating healthily because you may be tempted to "go along with the crowd" in skipping breakfast, eating too much junk or not eating regularly. It will be up to you to make the right choices so that you will have enough energy for the trip activities and to keep yourself feeling reasonably well. Sometimes this may mean speaking out about eating better. Sometimes you may need to choose different friends for meals that are on your own. You may need to plan on more snacks if you feel you will need them and you know your friends won't be stopping for snacks.

Here are a few hints you might want to try:

- Eat breakfast, even if you don't normally. Housing provided breakfasts usually are buffet style so you should be able to choose what you want. Be sure to have something to drink, juice is great; you need to start off the day well hydrated. If you need coffee or tea try to at least eat something with it. If there is a protein provided: eggs, meat, cheese, try to eat at least a little. These will digest more slowly and give you more energy later in the morning. Toast, pancakes, rolls, are great for energy. Cereal is good too, but try to eat something a little substantial: cheerios, granola, oatmeal, instead of sugar coated ones that will just give you quick energy then cause you to feel weak later. If you must eat these try to eat some protein too. Sometimes there will be fruit provided. You may be able to take a piece with you to have later.

- If breakfast is early you may want to have a midmorning snack. Granola bars, trail mix, peanuts, water, juice, may tied you over until lunch.

- Try not to wait too long for lunch, if possible. You may be on your own for lunch so if you can, try a local café or restaurant, instead of the nearest McDonald's. Try the local cuisine. Eat a filling lunch with protein: meat, chicken, cheese, and a beverage.

- Mid-afternoon snacks and beverages will keep you going until dinner. If it is really hot try to stay away from too much pop, it is really dehydrating. Juice, lemonade, and fruit slushes can be quite refreshing. Additional bottled water is great too.

- Eat a balanced dinner with plenty of water.

- You may be hungry later in the evening too. Try to stay away from too much caffeine. Water is great. Try not to eat too much sugar. If you are really hungry try to eat some protein too: peanuts, cheese.

- One of the most important things you can to is to drink plenty of liquids, especially water. If you have a sensitive stomach you may need to drink bottled water.

- Try to eat at the opportunities you are given, even if you are not hungry. You never know when your next meal may be; sometimes schedules get changed.

- Always have snacks and a bottle of water with you wherever you go!!!

ATTITUDE IS EVERYTHING

The key to an enjoyable trip will lie with your attitude. No matter what happens on your trip you are still in control of your attitude. You need to remember that you are a guest in another country, or another part of your own country. Your trip will go a lot better if you go into the experience with an open mind, excited to learn about different cultures, people, and lifestyles, with a willingness to broaden your perspectives. If you think only America, or your State for that matter, is right, best, most developed, and you continually criticize the "strange" customs, cultural differences, language, money, food, houses, plumbing, then you will be considered an "Ugly American", and may be treated as such. Ask your Travel Agent about any cultural differences that you need to be aware of, such as pointing fingers or gestures that might be offensive to that culture.

To really get so much more out of your trip you need to go into it with an attitude of willingness to appreciate the similarities and differences between the cultures you are visiting and your own. Try to be genuinely interested in the people and cultures that you visit. Try some new things out of your comfort zone while you are there. Local cuisine is a good example. If at all possible try to eat at least a few meals at local restaurants with only a small group of people and try the local menu.

Accept and try to understand why things are done differently than you are used to. There are usually good reasons that you may not be able to see. Be observant and sensitive to the "atmosphere" of the sights you are visiting. This is especially true in churches, cathedrals and museums. These are not the places for loud talking and laughing. Be sensitive in how you dress too. Skirts and nicer clothes (than jeans) may be more acceptable in certain places: cathedrals, theatre and nice restaurants.

If you are in a foreign country with a language different than yours, even if English is spoken, but with different words than you are used to, try to make an attempt at communicating with the people there. Do not make fun of the language, or the "strange words", just enjoy the diversity. Keep your language phrase book handy and don't say, "everyone should just speak English". Most of the countries you will be visiting, and their languages, have been around longer than America has.

Some things may seem extremely strange to you: children begging on the streets, people selling things everywhere, having to bargain for the best price, foreign money in coins with higher denominations than you are used to, no ice in drinks. Just take it all in and not be judgmental. Their life is very different from yours, not necessarily worse, or better.

There may be times when people are rude to you, pushing you aside, swearing at you, even openly criticizing the U.S. government to you, just because they recognize you as American. It is best not to take any of this too personally. Just realize that they have their opinion and they are usually reacting to other preconceived notions too. Try to be as polite as possible and go about your business.

Above all be positive and optimistic as much as possible. Focus on the good points of each place you are at. Don't dwell on the problems and especially **do not** compare things to "back home". Try to enjoy all the new things you are experiencing, and learn as much as possible.

CHAPTER 13 - RULES AND GUIDELINES

STUDENT GUIDELINES: RULES, BEHAVIOR AND MANNERS

Clear instruction for the students, staff, chaperones and parents as to the rules, specific guidelines for behavior and appropriate manners that are expected to be followed by the entire group can really help your trip to be a very enjoyable one. All these need to be explained to the entire group, including parents, and any consequences for misbehavior need to be outlined carefully. It is important to print these out and make sure everyone going on the trip has a copy, as well as each set of parents.

The following are suggested rules and guidelines for appropriate behavior. You may need to change or add to some of these to fit your specific group. Some of these suggestions may seem simplistic, or very obvious, but remember that for some of your students this may be their first flight, or their first experience with a tour bus, and probably a lot of them have never stayed in a hotel room with their friends and without their parents. It is quite possible that these experiences may be firsts for some of your chaperones too, especially if this trip is an international one.

Rules

If this is a school-sponsored trip then usually all the school rules and expectations for that school are in effect **at all times** for the entire trip. School specified consequences will occur also. Be sure that everyone, especially the students and parents, understand this.

General rules that will apply to students include:

- No use of alcohol, tobacco, or illegal drugs at any time
- No members of the opposite sex in anyone's room at any time
- Be in your room at the specified bed-check time and stay there until the wake-up time
- Always be with at least one other person at all times
- Public displays of affection should be limited to holding hands, maybe arms on shoulders, but always sitting upright in the seats. A quick kiss goodnight may be acceptable but no long embraces and kisses

Guidelines for Behavior and Manners

Always be courteous to everyone all of the time. This includes fellow students, chaperones, instructors, bus drivers, and anyone else that you come in contact with. Remember that as soon as you leave on the trip you are not "your own" but you are representing your school, your hometown, your state and your nation. You will be judged by all you meet and they will assume that you represent the accepted behavior at your school, hometown, state and nation. Ask your Travel Agent about specific customs that you need to know: tipping amounts and when expected, telephone procedures.

If a student does have a disagreement with a chaperone, or feels that they were treated unfairly, they should still treat the chaperone with respect and courtesy, maybe explaining the situation a little. But they still need to abide by the chaperone's direction or decision. Afterwards they can then go to the Leader and discuss the situation.

Above all, remember that you will be seeing and experiencing a new area of your own country or other countries, with many new sights, cultures and history. You may not see these again so you might as well stay awake and enjoy it all as much as possible. Keep as positive an attitude as you can. This will make all the difference in the world for you to have an enjoyable trip.

In the Airport

- Listen carefully and follow all instructions
- Stay with the group at all times unless instructed otherwise, your group may be asked to move to a specific place and you need to be there to hear directions
- Always ask permission if you need to leave the group: restroom, eat, shop; you may be allowed to leave the group for awhile if you have a long wait
- If going to the restroom, or **anywhere**, always have at least one other person with you
- Keep track of any luggage you have with you, especially daypacks
- Be careful of your comments when going through the metal detectors and with any searches…this is serious business
- Have your picture identification and/or Passport ready at check-in, with luggage keys handy

On the Airplane

- Follow all directions given by flight attendants and be courteous to everyone
- Don't change seats unless all those involved agree
- Do not tilt your seat back without asking the passenger behind you if they would be comfortable with it, and then just a little

- Remain in your seat at all times, except when you need to get up to use the restroom or to take a short walk around the plane; once an hour is enough
- Keep your seat belt fastened at all times (this is very important if turbulence is encountered; a sign will light up if it is mandatory at any time)
- Don't yell or talk loudly (many people will be sleeping during the flight)
- Keep your daypack with you, under the seat when necessary Don't get into the overhead storage bins during the flight
- Have something to drink whenever it is offered, water, pop, juice. Go easy on beverages with caffeine in them Ginger ale is good for a queasy stomach
- Chew gum or suck on hard candy during the flight, the air can be very dry
- Take your contacts out if your eyes become very dry, you don't want to have problems later
- If you want to use your CD player remember you cannot use it during take-off and landing
- Try to eat whatever is provided for you unless you just can't stand it, you may not get another meal for awhile
- Try to sleep a little, especially if it is a long flight; earplugs and a sleep mask can really help
- Do not call the flight attendants unless you really need something…they are not your personal servants

On the Bus

- Sit facing forward, no climbing on seats
- Do not tilt your seat back without asking the passenger behind you if they would be comfortable with it, and even then only tilt it back a little
- You may use headphones to listen to your CD's, talk or play video games except when a tour guide is describing sights or you are receiving instructions
- You need to stay awake as much as possible to see the sights on any tour; during long trips you may be given the opportunity to sleep
- Stay in your seat except when retrieving something from the overhead bins
- Keep the same seat if you are asked to do so throughout the trip
- Talk softly, don't yell
- Speak up to the chaperones if someone is missing or ill or if something may have been overlooked accidentally

- Remain seated and quiet when the bus has arrived at your destination so you will be able to hear any instructions from chaperones and leaders
- If you have a tour guide and he/she happens to say something about the history or culture of their country, and it doesn't seem to agree with what you have been taught, don't challenge them. Realize that they have been taught from the perspective and politics of their country. Remember that this is a learning experience, and not all countries are as pro USA as we are.

In Hotels and Hostels

- Be courteous to all other guests
- Do not open the door without asking who is on the other side
- Be quiet, no yelling and no running, anywhere
- No congregating in the halls, there are other guests in the housing too, go down to the lounge areas for socializing
- Be in your room at bed-check time and stay in there until wake-up time
- Don't stay up late talking or watching movies, you'll regret it the next day
- Take care of the furniture and equipment in your room, keep it as clean as possible (garbage in the garbage can)
- Leave a tip for a stay longer than two days if instructed by your Travel Agent (customs vary)
- Keep your money, wallet and money belt put away in your luggage when you are not carrying them

Dining Rooms and Restaurants

- Remove any hats or caps while seated
- Be mindful of the amount of time you have to eat, small groups get served faster than large ones
- Try the local cuisine, this is one of the reasons why you came
- Tip in the appropriate amount

Home stays

- Be polite and courteous to your "Home stay family" at all times
- Make your bed and hang up any towels you use
- Eat, or at least try, the food that is prepared for you
- Leave a thank you card and/or gift at the end of your stay
- Report any problems to the leader

Tours and Sightseeing

- Stay with the group at all times unless instructed otherwise
- When not with the large group **always** be with at least one other person
- Always carry with you a copy of your Passport, medical card and medical history
- Listen to all instructions and follow them
- Be extra mindful of your possessions: camera, clothes, money; you don't want to leave them anywhere
- Be aware of the amount of time you have at a sight; allow yourself enough time to visit the gift shop, restroom, before returning to your designated meeting area on time
- Be polite to all you come into contact with
- If you are tired don't whine and complain, everyone else is tired too

CONSEQUENCES

Most of the inappropriate behavior you see by students will only need a gentle reminder or just a stern look to cause a change to the right kind of behavior. However, sometimes more action will be required. Consequences should be discussed beforehand with the entire group, especially with all the parents. It is usually helpful to have a progression of consequences too, if the inappropriate behavior does not stop. Possible consequences could include:

- A reminder that the behavior is inappropriate
- Another reminder if necessary, with the suggestion that if the behavior doesn't improve it will need to be discussed with the Leader of the group
- A discussion with the Leader and/or chaperone about the behavior and what kinds of changes are expected
- A call home to parents, with the Leader present, explaining the situation
- A student may be directed to spend all their time with adult chaperones if the behavior does not improve
- If a student is continually late ask them to be 15 minutes early the next time
- If a student is late for bed-check have them spend the next night's "free time" in their room, without visitors
- If a student is rude to a chaperone or other adult, or another student, an apology may be needed
- If several students misbehave they may need to miss an activity, even stay on the bus for a certain period of time

- however, at least two adults would need to stay with them

- Gross disobedience of the specific rules for the trip or extreme inappropriate behavior may result in the student being sent home at the parent's expense (this may be difficult to enforce if you are in a foreign country)

In any case you will want to hear the whole story, especially the student's version. Sometimes there are plausible explanations for certain indiscretions. For example, a student may be late for bed-check because he was in the lobby at a public phone calling home. The line may have been long and he couldn't get to the phone until 10:55. By the time he called home and came back upstairs to his room it was 11:10. Ten minutes past bed-check. You could probably understand this if the whole group had arrived at 10:30 or so, and only had a short time until bed-check. However, if the group had been there over an hour or so the student probably just waited until the last minute to get in line for the phone.

The purpose of consequences is to keep the behavior from occurring again, either by that particular student, or 10 others the next night who will then think that they can "get away with it". Do remind everyone that it is very important for anyone not to be late because that makes the **whole group** late and may even disrupt the schedule and possibly cause everyone to miss a special event or arranged tour.

INAPPROPRIATE BEHAVIOR BY CHAPERONES

Inappropriate behavior from chaperones, instructors, or other adults on the trip may be a little harder to deal with. The Leader of the group may be the one who will have to deal with this because ultimately he or she is responsible for the whole group. The Leader will need to discuss any inappropriate behavior with the person privately, and explain how the behavior is not a good example to set for the whole group.

Hopefully, that will be all that is needed. If the behavior continues to be a concern, for example: continually yelling at the students, treating the students or others harshly, violating specific chaperone rules such as drinking or smoking in front of students, the Leader may want to gather a few adults together and talk to the person again, in a private setting.

Emphasizing that everyone needs to set a good example for the students and that adults have a special responsibility to do this on the trip may help. Also, a reminder that the chaperone did sign an agreement (if they did) to behave in a certain way and they need to stick to it.

Sometimes adults may simply not have the patience to deal with the students when they, themselves, become stressed and tired out by the hectic schedule of the trip. There may come a time that the chaperone may need to be relieved of chaperoning responsibilities for a certain period of time to help improve the situation.

These kinds of situations can be very difficult experiences for everyone so the Leader, and all those adults involved, must handle things very carefully and with great discretion. However, the safety and well being of the students **must** come first in all situations like this, so these concerns need to be dealt with.

Sometimes several of the adults may be getting very stressed and tired so decisions may need to be made to slow the schedule down some and allow more time for everyone to get a little more rest and relax a little. If a lot of the adults are getting too tired then the students probably are too.

PART THREE: PARTICIPATING IN THE TRIP

CHAPTER 14 - THE TRIP

PRE-TRIP PREPARATIONS

The following is a suggested timetable and a schedule of things to do to prepare for your trip. The suggestions follow the "*Action Plans*" that were listed in the planning portion of this book. You may need to adjust this timetable to fit the length of time you have to prepare for a trip as well as adding or eliminating things you need to do depending on what kind of trip yours is. This particular schedule is designed for an international trip. You can eliminate some of the items if your trip is within the United States.

Trip Countdown Calendar

12 Months Before Trip
- Decide you are going on the trip
- Begin saving money toward all the costs of the trip

11 Months
- Begin thinking about the items you will need for the trip

10 Months
- Begin buying needed items: film, batteries

9 Months
- Continue to save money and buy needed items

8 Months
- Consider clothes needed for the trip, watch for sales

7 Months
- Decide on buying Trip/Travel Insurance

6 Months
- Have Passport picture taken, get birth certificate and apply for Passport
- Obtain Picture Identification Card if needed
- Make copies of Passport ID page and Picture Identification Card when available
- Check over luggage and buy or borrow needed items

5 Months
- Begin gathering needed travel items and first aid supplies
- Check over clothes again, purchase needed items
- "Trial Pack" everything to see if it will fit in luggage

4 Months

- Think about a Trip Budget and how you want to deal with your Trip money
- Discuss trip finances with parents
- Check expiration dates on credit cards and ATM cards
- Practice with the camera you want to take
- Fill out Special Power of Attorney and have it notarized

3 Months

- Begin gathering items for carry-on bag, daypack
- Fill out index cards with needed account and phone numbers
- Fill out luggage tags and information cards for each piece of luggage
- Fill out medical information card for money belt
- Fill out Medical Release Form and Medication Form
- Discuss with parents medical concerns and medications

2 Months

- "Trial Pack" the clothes and other items you want to take
- Buy or borrow additional clothes and items you will need
- "Break in" any shoes you are taking on the trip
- Buy various sizes of ziplock bags

1 Month

- Get a haircut
- Order any foreign currency that you will need

2 Weeks

- Begin packing your carry-on bag and daypack
- Put identifying marks on all your luggage
- Take pictures of all the things you are taking
- Take pictures of all the pieces of luggage you are taking

1 Week

- Pack your suitcase and finish packing carry-on, daypack
- Pack money belt, wallet

2-3 Days

- Buy snacks, bottled water, magazines
- Check over lists to see if you have forgotten anything

1 Day

- Put Driver's License, Picture Identification in wallet

During the last two weeks before the trip the travelers will have many other responsibilities that they will need to take care of. The students may have tests to study for as well as projects to finish. They may even have additional homework to do if they will be missing days of school. Adults that are going will have to be taking care of any household duties that will need to be done while they are gone: paying bills, arranging for pets, buying extra food for those staying at home. This all puts extra pressure on everyone at this time, so careful planning, and having as much done ahead of time as possible will really help ease some of the stress.

Pre-Trip Meeting

A few days before the departure date of the trip you should have a final trip meeting. At this meeting copies of the final itinerary should be handed out to all those going on the trip and to the parents staying home. Phone numbers of the Travel Agency and all the housing sites, as well as any cell numbers (if they will have service) of the Leader and chaperones should be on the itinerary.

If Passports are needed, the Leader may opt to carry the students' Passports to the airport in order to insure that they are all there at check in time. If this is the case the Passports should be turned into the assigned chaperone during the small group meeting. The chaperone can then put them in a labeled ziplock bag and give them to the Leader. It will be much easier for the Leader to hand them out again at the airport by simply handing all the ziplock bags back to the chaperones to then hand the Passports out to the students. The label can have the chaperone's name on it and all the names of the students assigned to that particular chaperone.

This is also the time for the Leader to hand out all the copies of Passports, picture ID's, lists of students, and lists of bus assignments and roommate assignments, to the assigned chaperones. There may also be additional brochures, maps and papers that the Travel Agent may provide for the entire group that should be handed out to everyone at this time.

Specific information about the departure day should be printed up also and carefully gone over during the meeting. The exact location you will be leaving from (south parking lot of the high school) and times for checking in, loading and leaving need to be stressed. Also, information on the return schedule and when, where and what time everyone will need to be picked up at the end of the trip. There should be a list of things that the assigned chaperone will ask each of their students to make sure that they have with them on departure day. These items could be their Picture Identification and/or Passport, if needed; money, ATM card, and luggage tags on each piece of luggage. They need to understand that they will have to show all of these things to their assigned chaperone when they check in with their chaperone on departure day.

There should also be plenty of time allowed for a question and answer time for those last minute questions and concerns. After all the questions have been answered the assigned small groups should meet.

This is a good time for the assigned chaperones to meet with their assigned students and their parents and discuss with them the listed items. It would be helpful to "touch base" as to how they have dealt with these areas as a family and to talk about any concerns the parents want the chaperones to know about. Chaperones need to ask the parents if the students have all the needed items, what arrangements have been made for money, and what concerns they have about their students in the various areas. Remind parents that the chaperones are not simply being curious but need to know if their assigned students are adequately prepared for the trip and if there are concerns they need to know about to adequately chaperone the students.

Chaperone/Parent/Student Discussion List

Travel Documents

- Passport, if needed
- Picture Identification Card***
- Medical Information: Insurance Policy #; Dr. Phone #

Money Information

- Cash being carried: American, foreign***
- ATM Card: account # and emergency # to call if lost***
- Credit card: account # and emergency # to call if lost
- Budget Plan

Personal Information

- Carried in money belt, wallet: Parents name, address, phone #; other emergency numbers
- Luggage tags filled out completely for each bag***
- Carried in suitcases: Name, address and phone #; copy of Passport page

Personal Information to Be Discussed With Parent

- Special medical concerns
- Medications carried by student***
- Budgeting concerns
- Other information

***Will be checked by chaperone on Departure Day

THE TRIP

Departure Day

If everyone is leaving on the same flight, or flights, at least within an hour or two of each other, you will probably all be able to leave from "home" at the same time. If not, you may have to have separate check in times at "home" and then check in at the airport in separate groups at separate times.

The airline may request that the group check in at the airport for an international flight at least three hours, or more, before the flight leaves. For a continental flight it may be two hours. With the additional security now you may need additional time, especially with a large group. Be sure to allow enough time so the group will not be rushed.

Here is a suggested schedule for a departure day with two flights leaving within 45 minutes of each other. Everyone leaves "home" at the same time. The times are given for the departure day and the beginning of the first tour day as suggestions and estimations for the amount of time each activity takes.

SAMPLE SCHEDULE

Leaving Home

8:00AM Only adults, students of chaperones and students helping load buses arrive at departure site

8:15AM Chaperones receive student check off list from Leader
- Chaperones place their large pieces of luggage by luggage bays of their assigned bus
- Chaperones board buses and choose their seats, leaving carry-ons on seats
- Chaperones check off students that are there at that time
- Students check in with their assigned chaperones then place their luggage by their assigned buses and board the buses to choose their seats
- Student luggage loaders begin loading luggage in luggage bays after they have checked in and chosen their seats

8:30AM All other students begin arriving
- Students check in with assigned chaperone, then move luggage to their assigned bus luggage bays

- Students board buses and choose their seats
- Luggage loaders continue loading luggage until all is loaded

8:45AM Chaperones turn in check in list to Leader after all their assigned students have arrived and checked in with them

- Students are instructed to say their good-byes and board the buses at this time
- Chaperones board buses if all their students are there and checked in

8:55AM Chaperones do count of travelers on buses and report number to Leader

- Leader does final check and gives any additional instructions to each bus if necessary

9:00AM Buses depart for airport

Airport

9:50AM Buses arrive at airport and begin unloading

10:00AM Everyone brings all luggage into airport and to assigned area

- Leader checks in group and lines everyone up for individual check in, spreading chaperones throughout the line. Passports may be handed out at this time.

10:10AM Everyone begins to check in at ticket counter, answering questions, showing their Passport and/or Picture Identification and checking their large luggage

- After check in individuals proceed to security checkpoint, placing their carry-on in x-ray machine and walk through metal detector and continue on to departure gate
- Everyone needs to keep moving and not wait around for a group of their friends

10:50AM Everyone arrives at departure gate and congregates in one area. Students check in with chaperones and wait for instructions

11:00AM Everyone is instructed to leave their carry-ons, etc. in one area and to go **nearby** to get lunch, use the restroom, etc., taking turns so there are always people there to "guard" the luggage

12:00 Noon Everyone returns to departure gate area and students again check in with chaperones

12:15PM Leader and chaperones divide up tickets and hand them out to groups of 2, 3, 4 and 5 according to flights. Chaperones may choose first. Be sure to separate groups for separate flights first! You may want chaperones to gather Passports from students at this time, and return them on the plane before landing, or you may let them keep them with them.

12:30PM Last minute trips to restroom, drinking fountain, etc. for Group # 1
(1:15PM) Last minute trips to restroom, drinking fountain, etc. for Group # 2

12:45PM Group # 1 prepares for boarding
(1:30PM) Group # 2 prepares for boarding
- Gather all luggage items together, getting into seating groups

1:00PM Group # 1 is called for boarding
(1:45PM) Group # 2 is called for boarding
- Once on plane find seat and place carry-on in overhead luggage bin or under seat
- Sit down and get settled, putting on your seat belt
- Do not use your CD Player or electronic games until seatbelt sign is off after plane is in flight
- Do not try to change seats while others are boarding the plane

Flight

1:20PM Group # 1
(2:05PM) Group # 2
- Listen to all instructions from flight attendants

1:30PM Take Off - Group # 1
(2:15PM) Take Off - Group # 2
- Keep seatbelt on and stay seated until seatbelt sign goes off

1:45PM Group # 1
(3:00PM) Group # 2

Once seatbelt sign is off you may take off your seatbelt but **it is recommended to keep it on all times in case of turbulence**

- You may get up to use the restroom but it is best to stay seated most of the time
- Flight attendants may start beverage service
- Be sure to have something to drink

Both Flights: Time to talk with your seatmates, read, play games, write,

- A meal, or two, may be served during the flight...be sure to at least try to eat a little because it may be awhile until your next meal
- Be sure to have something to drink every time something is offered
- Walk around a little every hour if possible
- If it is a long flight try to sleep a little
- When it is nearing time for landing the flight attendants will tell you; gather all the items you have used during the flight and place them in your carry-on; put your seatbelt on
- After landing and you are gathering your carry-ons be sure to check your seat to make sure nothing has fallen between the cracks

Arrival

Both flights Group # 1 arrives first, 35 minutes later Group # 2 arrives

- After leaving plane have group congregate together and students check in with chaperones
- Show Passports as they pass through Immigration
- Chaperones collect Passports from students
- When everyone is accounted for each group heads for the baggage claim area
- Once there the group needs to find an area to gather
- Group # 1 will choose the area, Group # 2 will find them when they arrive
- Students with job of luggage retrieval stand near carousel and grab luggage that is marked with yarn for the group; others may slide the luggage to the area where the group is
- Everyone claims their bags and stands with their luggage waiting for the rest of the group to get their luggage
- Instruments, uniform boxes, and other supplies may be retrieved at this time too
- Any lost luggage or other lost items need to be reported to airport personnel

- The Leader will need to check on the transportation to the housing site…a representative from the Travel Agency may meet you and assist you with boarding the buses
- After everyone has their luggage and other items the group should proceed to the transportation provided
- If the bus set up is similar to the assigned tour buses have the members of the group go to their assigned bus (1,2 or 3). This will help in determining if everyone is on the buses
- Luggage should be placed near the luggage bays and luggage loaders should begin loading the luggage; loaders should have already placed their daypack, etc. on their seat on the bus
- After everyone is on the bus counts should be taken to see if everyone is there

Housing Site

Buses arrive at the housing site; luggage unloaders unload luggage from luggage bays; everyone retrieves their own luggage and takes it into the housing site

- Leader checks in with the housing site and receives room assignments and keys, arranges for wake up calls if possible
- The housing site may, or may not, have made person assignments to the rooms; if not, the Leader will need to look over the room assignments and determine where the chaperones should be and how to separate the boys and girls (separate floors are great but the housing site may not have given them to you)
- The group should be in an area of the lobby by themselves if possible, so the room assignments can be given out in a quiet setting
- Have the chaperones write down the room assignments as the Leader calls them out
- Have one representative from each room assignment come up to get the keys
- You may want everyone to wait until everyone has received their assignment before they find their rooms (it can get very noisy and confusing if half the group is moving around)
- Give bed-check times and other instructions concerning the activities for the rest of the day, arrangements and times for meals and details for the next morning: wake-up time, breakfast time, loading and departure time

Bed-check

11:00PM Students should be in their rooms for the night at this time. Chaperones go to their assigned students' room, knock, and go in to see that each student is actually there, and there are no extras; encourage them to go to sleep soon

- At this time the security procedures for the night should be in place: hired guards, or chaperones and/or other adults patrolling the halls; possibly pieces of tape may be placed in 2 spots on the doors

Rest of Trip

7:00AM Wake up calls or someone from the group knocks on the doors of each assigned room; make sure someone answers the door; at least 90 minutes before scheduled time to load the buses

7:30AM Breakfast may be at the housing site, or at nearby restaurants

8:30AM Load buses

- Students check in with their chaperones before they board the buses; chaperones may have checked on them at breakfast, or at student rooms before to make sure that they are up
- Once buses are loaded counts are taken and confirmed with leader to check if everyone is there

8:45AM Buses depart for sightseeing, tours, performances

- Every time anyone leaves the bus and returns a count needs to be taken to make sure no one is left behind!!!

The scheduled itinerary is followed for the rest of the trip. Any problems and concerns are discussed with the Leader, Travel Agency representative, other adults and chaperones. It is really helpful for all the adults to have short meetings at the end of the day for discussion of any problems, changes to the itinerary, and suggestions for information to be given to the students for the next day's activities. This meeting needs to be short since the students will most likely be unsupervised at this time.

A meeting with the entire group could be held before this one with adults to reiterate some of the information to everyone at the same time. Synchronize watches so everyone has the same time.

If the group is moving to another housing site additional time may be needed to pack up and load the buses before leaving.

If there are instruments and uniforms boxes, they may need to be packed up more securely for the trip home. Time needs to be allowed for this.

The first few days of the trip everyone will be excited and usually pretty tolerant of one another. Then everyone may be getting physically tired and a little tired of being around so many people, or just certain people. Some may be getting irritable with those around them and there may be some relationship problems. Hopefully the itinerary may have some relaxing times built in at this time, so everyone can get a little more rest. This also might be a good time to encourage everyone to spend time with others on the trip.

Flight Home

The flight home should be very similar to the departure flight except if it is an international flight. If it is, sometime during that flight the flight attendants will hand out Customs Declaration Forms. Every traveler needs to fill out one of these before the plane lands. Even though some students may have their parents on the trip as chaperones they should still fill out their own form. This is where they will need to write down the value of the items they bought on the trip. Anything over $400 in value will be taxed at 10%, up to $1000 in value. The Customs Official will determine anything over that amount and the tax.

After leaving the plane everyone will walk through Immigration and Customs. Each person will need to show their Passport at Immigration and then present their Customs Declaration Form. If any tax is owed it will need to be paid at that time.

Arrival Home

Everyone will be excited to get home and tell everyone about the trip, but at the same time they will be a little disappointed that the trip is over. After everyone arrives at the "home site" students need to tell their chaperones when they are ready to leave with their parents. Chaperones then need to tell the Leader when all their students have left with their parents. The chaperone and/or the Leader will need to wait until every student has been picked up by their parents or other designated adult.

Arrangements need to be made for pick up of other instruments, uniform boxes and other shipping boxes that are not taken by the students or adults. You may need to have some sort of truck available to take them right then back to your school, or you may be able to arrange for some sort of storage at the airport until the next day when you can arrange for a truck.

THE DAYS AFTER THE TRIP

I have found that the days after the trip follow a rather predictable pattern. The first night after arriving everyone is really excited to share their experiences but at the same time may be extremely tired from the trip and the time changes. The next day everyone may just want to sleep, and think about the trip. They may be eager to unpack and show all their souvenirs and give out the gifts they have bought, or they may just want to wait until later.

If the time change has been more than 3 hours you may find yourself getting sleepy at different times and then wake up in the middle of the night. If usually takes about 1 day for every hour of time change to adjust back, if not more. Sometimes it can take a week or more until you have really adjusted back to "home" time.

Another thing I have noticed is that usually people are on an adrenaline high on the trip because they are very excited and constantly going and doing things. They may get pretty tired but they can usually keep going. Once they get home, and come down from the adrenaline high as they slow down, they may find themselves feeling extremely tired for a few days, and maybe a little down. The trip that they planned on for so long, maybe even over a year, is now over, and it is a bit depressing, even if they had a wonderful time. They don't need to despair...they will feel better soon, as long as they continue to take care of themselves: drinking plenty of fluids and getting a lot of sleep.

Unfortunately many travelers don't plan on this happening to them and don't allow themselves enough time to "recover" from the trip before they jump back into their busy activities.

It might be nice to have a group meeting of all those who participated in the trip, and their parents and friends, a few weeks after the trip. If people had double prints made of their pictures they could bring them to trade with others. Anyone that took videos of the trip might want to show them at this meeting. Everyone might want to bring souvenirs they bought to show everyone. There might be a time when those who want to can share some of their experiences on the trip and what they enjoyed the most with the rest of the group.

The Trip Committee should have a "wrap up" meeting to talk about the trip and what went really well and what changes they would like to make on another trip. Be sure someone writes all this down for future trips.

Again, I commend you on traveling with a group and I hope that you and everyone in your group has an absolutely wonderful trip!!!

APPENDIX: SAMPLE FORMS

The following applications, forms, checklists, calendars, as well as other items that are printed in the rest of the book are not intended, nor should be taken as legal advice. They are simply examples of forms, applications, checklists and other items that you may find useful in preparing for your trip. Please feel free to use and change them to fit your particular group and situation.

If you will be using any of the permission forms and/or using them to create your own: Trip Contract, Field Trip Permission Form, Medical Release Form, Authorization for Medication, Special Power of Attorney, be sure to consult an attorney for advice concerning your particular situation. You want to make sure you will be covered legally.

If your trip is a school sponsored one you will need to consult with the School District and their attorney concerning use of these forms on a school sponsored trip. They may, or may not, have forms of their own which they will want you to use.

TRIP COMMITMENT

_______________Trip
April 1 - April 8, 2002

(Student Name)________________________I am interested in going on the______________ (Band Trip?) to ____________________ on April 1 - April 8, 2002. The trip is contracted with the ____________Travel Agency and under the supervision of the ________________School District. I understand that the estimated cost of the trip is $1500 so far, which includes 14 meals. I will be responsible for any additional meals and other expenses (souvenirs, Passport, personal items)

I will pay the first payment of $200 that is due on September 10, 2001, and will pay the rest of the payments according to the prescribed payment schedule.

________________________(Student's signature)

Address____

Parent/Legal Guardian_____________________________Phone # ___________________

(Adult Name)________________________I am interested in chaperoning on the (Band Trip?) to ____________________on April 1 - April 8, 2002. I understand that the estimated cost will be the same as the students' cost of $1500. I am responsible for any additional expenses.

I will pay the first payment of $200 that is due on September 10, 2001, and will pay the rest of the payments according to the prescribed payment schedule.

______________________(Adult's Signature)

Address____

Student____Phone #________________________

TRIP CONTRACT

Student and Parental Agreement

I/we ______________________________give permission for ________________________to go
Parent/Legal Guardian Student

on the _______________________trip to ____________________from April 1 to April 8, 2002.

I__________________________and___________________________have read the Trip
Student Parent/Legal Guardian

Information and the Student Guidelines that we have been given and understand the guidelines, rules and expectations for this trip. We understand that these rules as well as all other ________________School rules, as well as those of the ________________School District will need to be followed on this trip. We understand that if the rules are not followed appropriate disciplinary action will be taken. Action could range from a reprimand, call home, and other consequences up to being sent home immediately at the parent's expense.

We also understand that the cost of this trip that has been arranged by the________________ _____________Booster Group is $1500. This includes payments to the_________________ ____________Travel Agency for airline, transportation, housing, arrangements and to the_________________Booster Group for other expenses (transportation to the airport, trip shirts, paperwork,) arranged for by the Booster Group. We agree to make the payments by the dates presented on the payment schedule. Any additional expenses: meals, Passport, travel expenses, souvenirs, are our responsibility.

________________________________ ________________________________

Student Signature Parent/Guardian Signature

Date____________________

____________________Travel Agency Information

____________________Trip to ______________________
April 1 - April 8, 2002

Ticketing Information:

______________________________ ______________________________ __________
Last Name (As on Passport) First Name (As on Passport) Middle Initial

____
Address

__________________________ _____________ _________________
City State Zip

____
Phone Number

________Male _______Female

FAA requires the following information:

___________________________________ __________________________
Next of Kin Phone Number

Airline and Hostel Information:

____
Special Dietary Needs

Frequent Flyer Information:

____ _____________________
Name of Airline Member ID Number

TRIP PAYMENT RECORD

________________________Name

Trip Insurance ________Date Paid $________Check #________

1st Payment due September 10 $200

__________Date Mailed $__________Check #________
__________Date Paid Treasurer $__________Deducted from Student Account

2nd Payment due October 10 $300

_________Date Mailed $_________Check #________
_________Date Paid Treasurer $_________Deducted from Student Account

3rd Payment due November 10 $300

________Date Mailed $_________Check #________
________Date Paid Treasurer $_________Deducted from Student Account

4th Payment due January 10 $200

________Date Mailed $________Check #________
________Date Paid Treasurer $________Deducted from Student Account

5th Payment due February 10 $300

_______Date Mailed $_______Check # ________
_______Date Paid Treasurer $_______Deducted from Student Account

6th Payment due March 1 $200

_______Date Mailed $_______Check # ________
_______Date Paid Treasurer $_______Deducted from Student Account

CALENDAR OF ITEMS TO BE TURNED IN

September

Turn in:

- ❑ Trip Commitment Form

October

Turn in:

- ❑ Trip Contract

November

Turn in:

- ❑ 2 Copies of Picture Identification Card

December

Turn in:

- ❑ 2 Copies of Passport ID Page

January

Turn in:

- ❑ Field Trip Permission Form
- ❑ Travel Agency Information Form
- ❑ Special Power of Attorney, **notarized**

February

Turn in:

- ❑ Medical Release and Consent to Treat Form
- ❑ Prescription and over-the-counter drug list

March

Turn in:

- ❑ Any additional forms

Items may be turned in before the month listed, but if they are not turned in during the month listed they will be considered to be late and subject to consequences. Discuss with the Group Leader if you have concerns about late forms.

ATTENDANCE SHEET FOR SMALL GROUPS

______________________________Small Group Leader's Name

The following students and parents were present at the Trip Meeting on____________________

Students	Parents
____________________	____________________
____________________	____________________
____________________	____________________
____________________	____________________
____________________	____________________
____________________	____________________
____________________	____________________
____________________	____________________

The following students and/or parents were not present at the meeting:

The following students have not turned in the listed required forms:

I have the following concerns about:

FIELD TRIP PERMISSION FORM

__________________SCHOOL DISTRICT

Informed Consent Form - District Curricular/Co-curricular/Interscholastic Activities

STUDENT NAME_______________________________**STUDENT #**__________

General Information **Date**__________________

The______________________________is planning a trip to______________________

The purpose of this trip is____

Trip Destination______________________________Phone #______________________

Address_______________________________Place of Lodging____________________

(enclose itinerary with further information if needed)

We will leave from___________________about (time)________on (date)____________

We will return to ____________________about (time)________on(date)____________

Itinerary is attached List of items needed is attached

Number Of Those Participating: # of Students______Minimum # of Adults_______

Type of Transportation

District Vehicle Commercial Transportation District Bus

Other (explain)____

****

Medical Information

The following health information should be noted:____________________________

____

Allergies to food, medications, bee stings, etc.___________________________________

The following medications, prescriptions, special diets, etc. are needed_______________

____

Medical Release

In the event of an accident or illness, I understand that reasonable effort will be made to contact the parent immediately. However, if I am not available, I authorized the school district representative or his/her designee to secure emergency medical care as needed.

Name of Preferred Doctor______________________________Phone #_______________

Name of Insurance Carrier_____________________________Policy #_______________

****

This activity provides a learning experience for the students and allows them an opportunity to apply their classroom learning. Although I understand that the school district will make reasonable effort to provide a safe environment, I am fully aware of the special dangers and risks inherent in participating in the activity. Being fully aware of the risks, I hereby give consent for (student)______________________to participate in the activity. My signature reflects knowledge of the details of the trip and the itinerary.

Parent Name_____________________________Address___________________________

Home Phone #____________________________Work Phone #______________________

Emergency Contact (Name & Phone #)_______________________________________

Signature of Parent/Guardian______________________________Date_______________

DEPARTURE DAY CHECK LIST

Chaperone___________________________

Student______________________________
Picture Identification
Money
ATM Card
Prescription or other drugs, if needed
Luggage tags

Student______________________________
Picture Identification
Money
ATM Card
Prescription or other drugs, if needed
Luggage tags

Student______________________________
Picture Identification
Money
ATM card
Prescription or other drugs, if needed
Luggage tags

Student______________________________
Picture Identification
Money
ATM card
Prescription or other drugs, if needed
Luggage tags

Student______________________________
Picture Identification
Money
ATM Card
Prescription or other drugs if needed
Luggage tags

Student______________________________
Picture Identification
Money
ATM Card
Prescription or other drugs if
Luggage tags

Student______________________________
Picture Identification
Money
ATM Card
Prescription or other drugs if needed
Luggage tags

Student______________________________
Picture Identification
Money
ATM Card
Prescription or other drugs if needed
Luggage tags

Student______________________________
Picture Identification
Money
ATM Card
Prescription or other drugs if needed
Luggage tags

Student______________________________
Picture Identification
Money
ATM Card
Prescription or other drugs if needed
Luggage tags

AUTHORIZATION FOR ADMINISTRATION OF MEDICATION ON A SCHOOL SPONSORED TRIP

Student Name:____Date of Birth____________

School____School District___________________

I request and authorize that the above-mentioned student be allowed to carry the following listed prescription and over-the-counter medications and to take them as ordered on the prescription container, or as needed for over-the-counter medications. Diagnosis and student's medical history is listed on the Medical Release Form. We have discussed the dosages for the conditions as needed. The doctor has discussed with said student the dosages and times and conditions under which prescription medications need to be taken. Student is aware of any side effects that may occur with the medications.

All medication, prescription and over-the-counter medication carried by the student will be in the original container, with instructions for use printed on the outside.

Prescription Medication

Name of Medication	Dosage	Times Given

Over-the-Counter Medication

Name of Medication	Dosage	Times Given

Name of Trip______________________________________Dates of Trip_________________

Signature of Parent/Guardian___________________________________Date______________

Telephone Number: Home:____________________Work:______________________

Cell:____________________E-mail_____________________

MEDICAL RELEASE FORM

Name______________________________Date of Birth____________Age_______
Student Adult
Address____

Parent/Legal Guardian___________________________Phone #____________________

EMERGENCY TELEPHONE NUMBERS
Work Phone: (Father)____________________(Mother)____________________

Emergency contact: (1)________________________(2)________________________
(Name & Phone #) (Name & Phone #)

MEDICAL INFORMATION
Prescription medication student must take on trip:_____________________________

Other medication student must take on trip:_____________________________________

Over-the-counter medication that student has parent permission to carry on trip and to take as needed. Parent has discussed with student dosage and indications where medication might be needed:____

____

Allergies to food, medications, bee stings, etc._____________________________________
Date of last tetanus shot:__________________________

Pertinent medical history and/or any chronic medical problems:____________________

____

MEDICAL INSURANCE
Medical Insurance Carrier:____________________________________

Name of Insured:__________________________Policy Number:__________________

MEDICAL RELEASE
In case of emergency and a parent cannot be reached by telephone, or I am incapacitated, I authorize the leader of this event, or his/her designee, to obtain medical treatment for my son/daughter, or myself, as needed. I also give permission for any hospital emergency department physician and/or member of the hospital medical staff requested by this physician to make examinations and provide medical and/or surgical treatment which in his or their judgement may be deemed necessary for my child's, or my own, health and welfare.

Signature_____________________________Signature_____________________________
(Parent/Guardian; Adult) (Student)

SPECIAL POWER OF ATTORNEY

KNOW ALL MEN BY THESE PRESENTS, that I ______________________________

do hereby make, constitute and appoint ______________________________

my true and lawful attorney for the sole and limited purpose to accompany my child on the trip

to __________________________. I hereby grant and give said attorney full authority and power to do and perform any and all acts necessary for the safety and well being of my child____________________ on this trip, as I might or could do if personally present.

This Special Power of Attorney shall began on ____________________the first day of the before mentioned trip and shall terminate on ____________________the last day of the trip, or until my child has been returned to me at the end of the trip.

Any person relying on this Special Power of Attorney may rely on a photocopy as if it were an original.

__________________________(Signature of Parent or Legal Guardian)

STATE OF ______________________)
) ss.
COUNTY OF ____________________)

Subscribed and sworn to before me this ____________________day of

____________________, ______________________.

____
Notary Public

My Commission Expires:

____

Information on Special Power of Attorney

The following is specific information pertaining to a Special Power of Attorney. Since laws vary from state to state and change over time be sure to have a lawyer review it before you use this document. If it is a school sponsored trip be sure to have the School District's lawyer look over the document too. Change the document as needed to fit your group and per your lawyer's suggestions.

- The person granting the Special Power of Attorney (the grantor) should sign the document before a notary. Notarizing a document allows it to be recorded in the public record and supports its authenticity.

- The grantor must **carefully instruct the agent** as to the needs of the child and their desires as to how the child should be treated.

- The grantor should instruct the agent as to any custodial arrangements with another parent, and inform the parent of this Special Power of Attorney being given. Sometimes in a divorce situation a parent may have been instructed not to leave the country with the child. The Special Power of Attorney gives limited custody of the child to the agent so then does not violate the custody agreement, unless the parent were to come on the trip.

- Be sure to limit the Special Power of Attorney to the **duration of time necessary.** This would start at the beginning, or first day of the trip, and continue on through the last day of the trip. You might want to add an additional line to continue the coverage up to the time the child has been returned by the agent to the parent, just in case the trip return is delayed for some unexpected reason.

- The agent authorized in the Special Power of Attorney should have access to the original document as needed, taking the original document on the trip only if the lawyer suggests this. Otherwise the grantor should have the original and give a copy to the agent to carry with them at all times on the trip. Be sure to consult with a lawyer on this issue!

SCHOLARSHIP APPLICATION

(__________________)Trip Scholarship Application

The (______________________________) is awarding ______(# Of) Trip Scholarships worth ________(amount) apiece. Every student anticipating on going on this trip is invited to apply for these Scholarships. Every applicant will be evaluated on several criteria, including, but not limited to: financial need, parent/student financial efforts towards trip, parent/student involvement in fund raisers, parent service and contribution to this group, year in school, as well as an essay on why this trip is important to them.

Once these Scholarships have been awarded the recipients will be asked to sign a Trip Commitment Form to declare that they will be going on this trip. They will also be asked to pay the first deposit for the trip on the date it is due. The Scholarship may be used for any payments thereafter, but not the first one.

If there is any chance you will not be able to participate in this trip, even with the Scholarship, please do not apply.

Return the completed application to ______________________You may mail the application to them at ____If you have any questions, please call__________________________________The due date is______________Be sure to answer all the questions and be sure to include your essay.

Personal Information:

Grade Level_____________

Name__________________________________Phone # _______________________

Address____

Father's Occupation__________________________

Employer____________________________Annual Income $____________________

Mother's Occupation_________________________

Employer____________________________Annual Income $____________________

Number of dependent children in family_________

Number of other family members attending college________

Person(s) responsible for your trip expenses___________________________

Extra efforts (or sacrifices) you or your family has made to help finance this trip:

____

____

____

Are there any other financial factors that you feel should influence our decision?

____

____

____

What, if any, fund-raisers have you been involved with, or plan on being involved with in the coming year (coupons, Auction, magazine sales, Entertainment Books)

____

____

____

What, if any, parent involvement and participation has there been or will be, for this Booster Group and their many activities:

____

____

____

ESSAY:

On a separate sheet of paper please write why this trip to____________________is important to you, and what you expect to learn from it.

I have read this statement and certify that this application, to the best of my knowledge, is true and correct.

______________________________ ____________________

Signature Date

Suggestions for Scoring Scholarship Applications

When the Trip Scholarship Committee for the group I was involved with did the evaluation of the Trip Scholarship Applications for the Band Trip to England they used a Scoring Guide. You may want to use something like this. This was simply a table set up with the various areas in columns: Financial Need (6), Parent/Student Financial Efforts towards Trip (4), Parent/Student Involvement in Fundraisers (3), Parent Service & Contribution to Band/Colorguard (3), Year in School (2) and the Essay (2). These different categories carried different "weights" as determined by the Committee and are shown in ( ). Each applicant was then given a score between 0 (low) up to 5 (high) in each category. This number was then multiplied by the "weight" given to each category and put in the Total area for that category. All these Totals for these categories were then added up for a final Total Score for each applicant.

We have found that the "weights" help to "level the playing field" somewhat for those who may, or may not, have a big financial need, and/or may be making sincere efforts to obtain the money needed for the trip. We also wanted to give priority to those students who were Juniors and Seniors and might not get a chance to go on another trip. They received 2 points while Underclassmen did not receive any points in that particular category. These may, or may not, be issues with your group.

The Trip Scholarship Committee met together and each member read the applications and then filled out a Scoring Guide giving each applicant the amount of points they thought each one should receive in each category and then multiplied these by the "weight". These Totals were then added up to reach the Total Score and they then shared these with the rest of the Committee. The Committee then discussed the Totals and the Essays and came to the decisions on who would receive the Scholarships.

The following is a suggested table. I left off some of the categories due to lack of space. The Essay area was very important in the decision making, especially when the scoring was close.

	Financial Need		Financial Efforts		Fundraisers		Year in School		
Weight	6		4		3		2		
	Points	Total	Points	Total	Points	Total	Points	Total	**Total**
# 1									
# 2									
# 3									

You may want to blank out the names on the applications and have them known only by numbers to the Committee Members if you wish. However, if the Committee members are at all familiar with the applicants they will guess who they are anyway.

After the decisions have been made on the recipients it is really nice for someone to call the recipients and inform them. Letters of Congratulations and Regrets should be sent to each of the applicants informing them of the Committee's decision also.

CHAIN OF COMMAND CHART

This is an example of a chart showing the "Chain of Command" that usually exists in a group trip, starting at the very top with the "Board of Directors" that may be over the group. This chart also shows the position of "Director" separately from the Leader, although many times the Director may want to be the Leader. Other times the Director may simply not have enough time to be the Leader in planning and arranging the trip and will want to delegate these responsibilities to another person, while still supplying input.

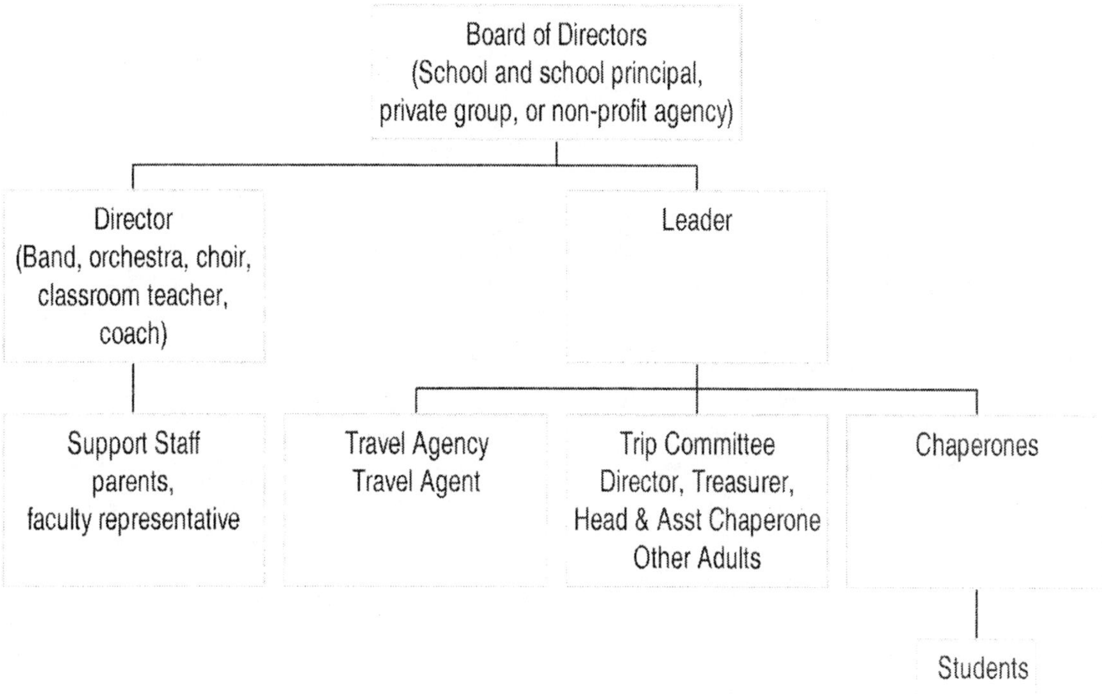

Job Descriptions:

Director: Responsible for performances; approves venues, itinerary; selects and organizes support staff; approves selection of Leader; member of Trip Committee; works closely with Leader and keeps he or she informed of needs for performances

Leader: Directs Trip Committee meetings (may, or may not, have vote in decisions); may voice opinions; sees that all bases are covered and that tasks are delegated and completed in a timely manner; serves as the **CONTACT PERSON** for all trouble shooting; liaison to parents and Travel Agency; sees that minutes are kept of meetings and are made available to the large group if requested; provides agendas for Trip Committee meetings and large group meetings

Trip Committee: May or not be chaperones on trip; has Treasurer and Fund Raising Chairman, if needed; selects Leader; meets on regular basis; members commit time for regular attendance and consensus building in decision making

TRAVEL AGENCY SELECTION GUIDE

When selecting a Travel Agency you will want to have certain parameters decided upon by the Trip Committee that you will give to the various Travel Agencies when you ask them to submit bids for your trip. You may, or may not, ask for a specific price range or for free trips at that particular time. Allow them to offer what they can and negotiate after you get the bids and/or have decided upon the Agency you want. Ask Agency to provide "Inspection Trip" for Leader, Director to "check out" housing, performances, tours to determine if suitable for students. This trip would occur 2 to 3 months before main trip so that minor changes could be made if needed.

DATES: Needs to be sometime between April 1 and April 20, but must include April 9-13

LENGTH OF TRIP: 9 to 10 Days 8 Nights (depending upon flights)

HOUSING: 3 to 4 Star Hotels; Hostels (only members of this group in rooms); University dorm rooms. Housing must include securely locked room for storage of instruments and be large enough to house entire group

CITIES AND SIGHTSEEING: London area, various cities near special sites: Warwick Castle; Stonehenge, Bath, Brighton; include a theater performance in London

MEALS: All Breakfasts
4 Lunches
3 Dinners
(Other meals may be provided on the flight or may be negotiated upon)

TOUR GUIDES: English speaking

INSTRUMENT TRANSPORTATION: Truck and driver for specified performance days

PERFORMANCES: At least 3 with suggestions from Agency

BUSES: Air conditioning and toilet on board

ROOM CHOICES AND CHARGES: Single (?) Double (10 to 15 rooms) 4 students/room (20 to 25 rooms) or other configurations as needed

GROUP SIZE: Price for 100 (80 students, 20 adults)
Price for 130 (100 students, 30 adults) as per discussion

TRIP CANCELLATION POLICY:

PAYMENTS: Schedule, Refunds, Credit Cards?

PAST EXPERIENCE WITH GROUPS LIKE THIS:

RECOMMENDATIONS FROM OTHER TOURS:

INDEX

ORDER FORM

"TRAVELING WITH GROUPS" ORDER FORM

Mail Check or Money Order To:	D and B Enterprises 11014 19th Ave. SE # 146 Everett, WA 98208
Ship To:	Name____________________ Address____________________ City____________State______Zip______

Phone #	(_____)__________________
Email Address	____________________

Quantity	*Item*	*Price*	*Total Price*
	Traveling With Groups	$14.95	$
	(State of Washington only)	Sales tax - 8.3%	$
		Shipping/Handling	$
		Subtotal	$
		TOTAL	$

Shipping and Handling: (all orders shipped USPS, unless otherwise requested) Allow 3 to 4 weeks for delivery. Please email for shipping and handling amount for orders over 5 books.

1 Book =	$4.95
2 Books =	$5.95
3 Books =	$7.95
4 Books =	$9.95
5 Books =	$10.95

Make checks/money orders payable to D and B Enterprises. Orders sent after check has cleared
.

Email questions to: donna@travelingwithgroups.net
Website: http://www.travelingwithgroups.net